HORTICULTURE NOTES I

Thomas Y. Wang

Spring 2019

HORTICULTURE NOTES I

Published by:
Mission Blue Project
San Francisco, California, USA

Send written correspondence to Mr. Wang at:
50 Frida Kahlo Way
EH/F Box 1
San Francisco, California 94112

ISBN 978-0-9840505-7-4
Published in the spring of 2019 after many days of rain

ISBN 978-0-9840505-7-4

90000

9 780984 050574

HORTICULTURE NOTES I
Spring 2019

SAFETY:
Watch out for passer-bys

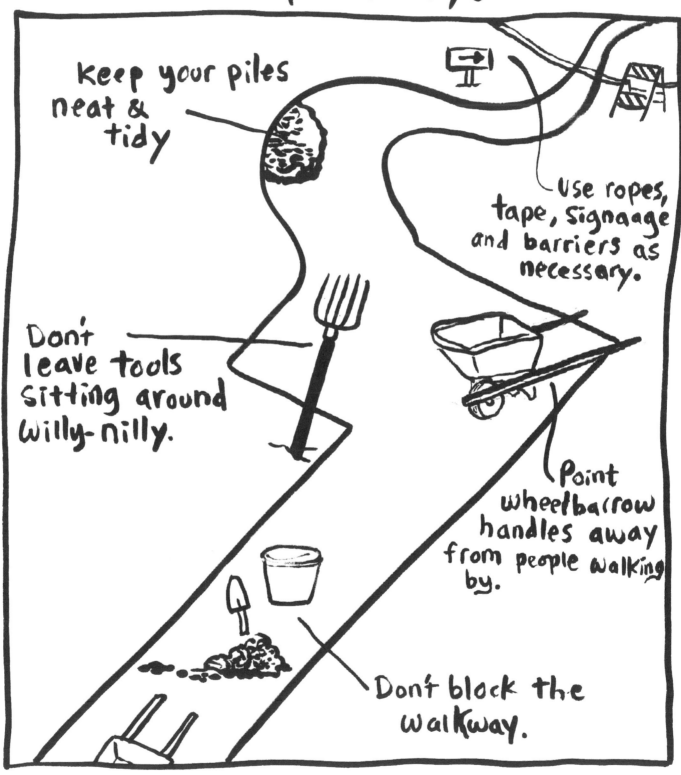

Keep your piles neat & tidy

Use ropes, tape, signaage and barriers as necessary.

Don't leave tools sitting around willy-nilly.

Point wheelbarrow handles away from people walking by.

Don't block the walkway.

SAFETY:

Keep your tools sharp:

Watch your step, be aware

Safety starts here:

Then here:

CAUTION!

Safety
Be extra careful —

Garden body mechanics - Weeding

Keep moving; don't stay in the same position

Alternate left & right, prone & squats

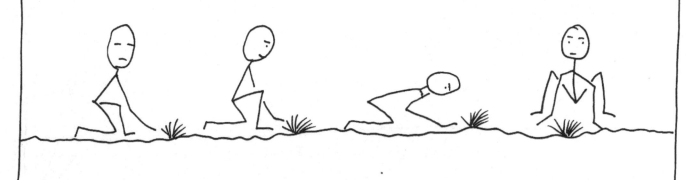

Keep back straight down into the core.
Bend from the core.

weed whole plants with roots when soil is loose & wet

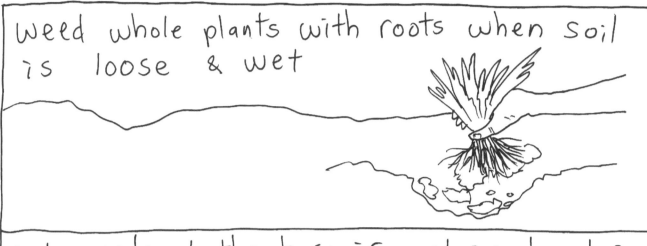

Cut weeds at the base if soil is hard & weeds are deep & persistent

Use tools for leverage & comfort

use fulcrums & supports

weeds are not your enemy. They are wild plants that like to be near people and follow us around. Kill some, then live and let live. Nature prefers diversity.

Garden body mechanics - Moving soil, rock, mulch

Small loads are easier to do all day long

Half full buckets

Small weight repetitions with the shovel

Turn with your loads - Head-torso-core down to your feet all together

Watch the twist

Back straight, use hips & legs to lift

Macho heroic loads will get you hurt

Steady & consistent loads will get the job done & keep you healthy

Garden body mechanics - pruning & cutting

Use the right tool

Keep it sharp.

Relax & let hands rest when engaged in repetitive tasks

500 more shoots to finish this tree

Keep the weight close to your core

STAY CENTERED.

PAIN!

Garden body mechanics - common injuries

CENTER OF DIVERSITY
CULTIVATED PLANTS OF TURTLE ISLAND

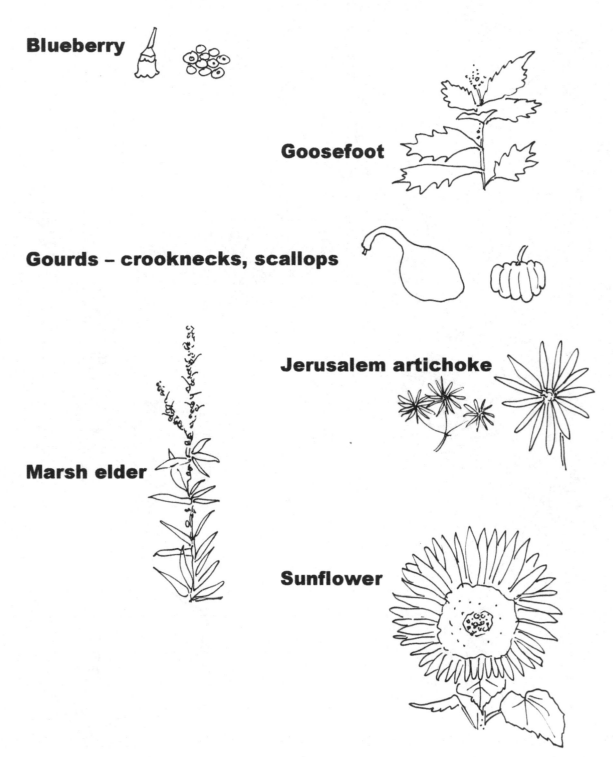

Blueberry

Goosefoot

Gourds – crooknecks, scallops

Jerusalem artichoke

Marsh elder

Sunflower

14

CENTER OF DIVERSITY
CULTIVATED PLANTS FROM THE SWAMPS OF THE EAGLE, PRICKLY PEAR, AND SERPENT

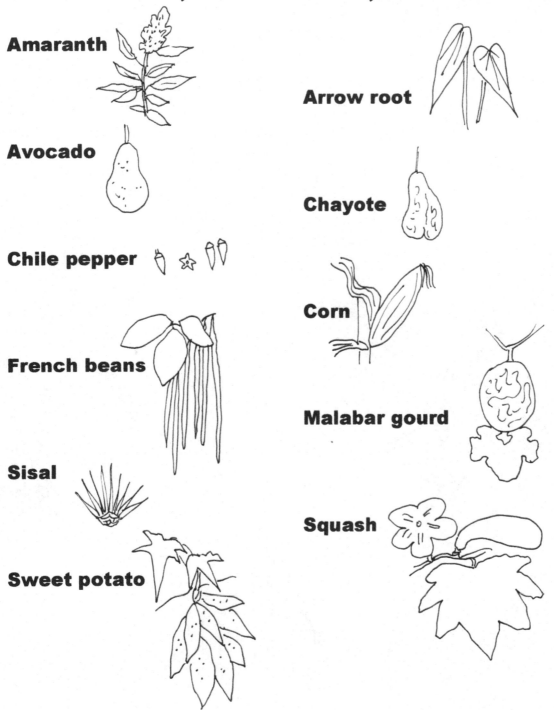

Amaranth

Avocado

Chile pepper

French beans

Sisal

Sweet potato

Arrow root

Chayote

Corn

Malabar gourd

Squash

CENTER OF DIVERSITY
CULTIVATED PLANTS OF THE
CONDOR HIGHLANDS & JAGUAR JUNGLES

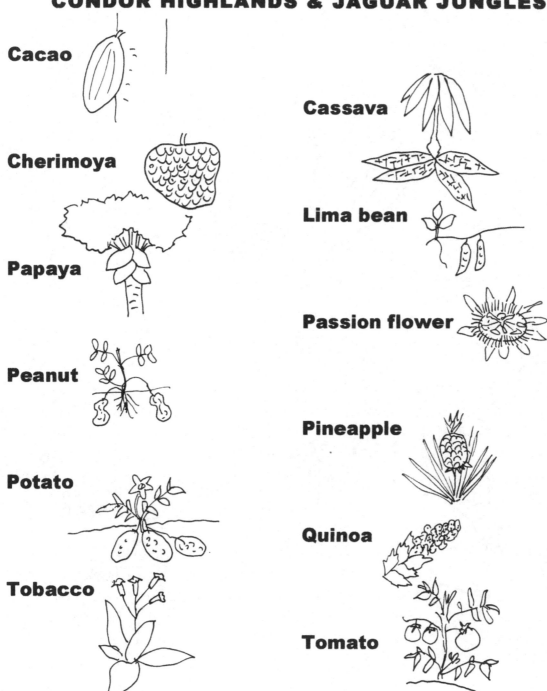

Cacao

Cherimoya

Papaya

Peanut

Potato

Tobacco

Cassava

Lima bean

Passion flower

Pineapple

Quinoa

Tomato

CENTER OF DIVERSITY
CULTIVATED PLANTS OF THE
SINDHU RIVER VALLEYS

Banana

Black pepper

Chickpea

Cucumber

Eggplant

Kenaf

Mango

Orange

Rice

Tamarindo

Taro

Yam

19

20

CENTER OF DIVERSITY
CULTIVATED PLANTS OF
THE ANCESTRAL HOMELAND

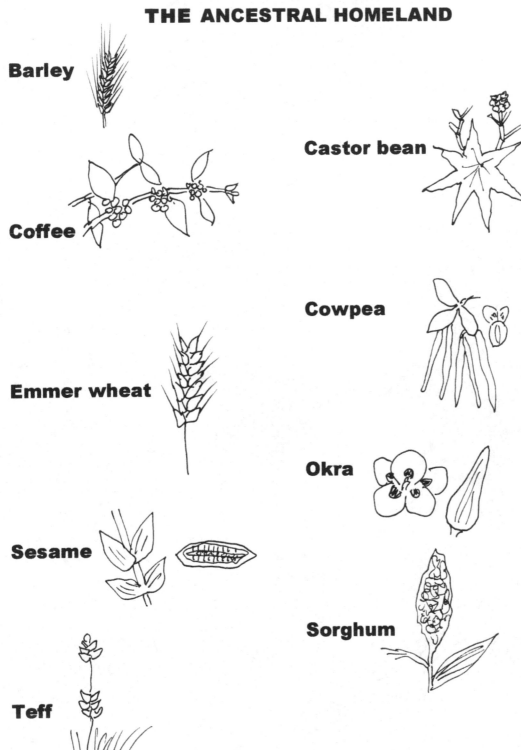

Barley

Coffee

Castor bean

Cowpea

Emmer wheat

Okra

Sesame

Sorghum

Teff

CENTER OF DIVERSITY
CULTIVATED PLANTS OF THE MIDDLE KINGDOM

Cherry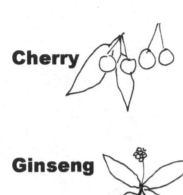

Chinese yam

Ginseng

Hemp

Litchi

Millet

Opium poppy

Peach

Soybean

Walnut

Velvet bean

CENTER OF DIVERSITY
CULTIVATED PLANTS OF GARUDA'S ARCHIPELAGOS

Breadfruit

Coconut

Job's tears

Mangosteen

Nutmeg

Pomelo

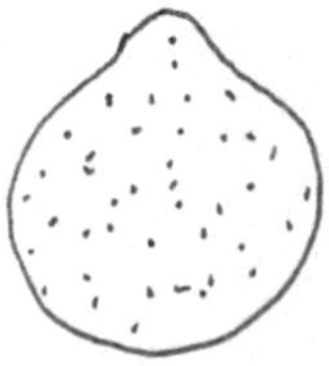

Sugar cane

26

CENTER OF DIVERSITY
CULTIVATED PLANTS OF DREAMTIME

Gumbi gumbi

Illwarra plum

Macadamia

Muntries

Quandong

Warrigal spinach

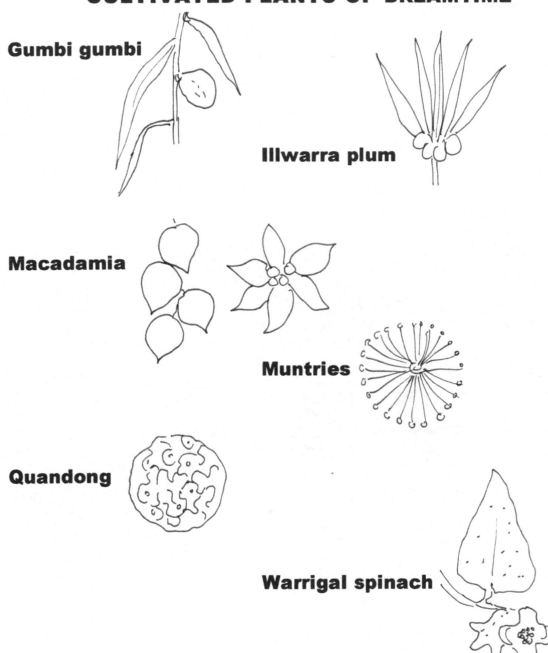

CENTER OF DIVERSITY
CULTIVATED PLANTS OF THE
CRADLE OF CIVILIZATION

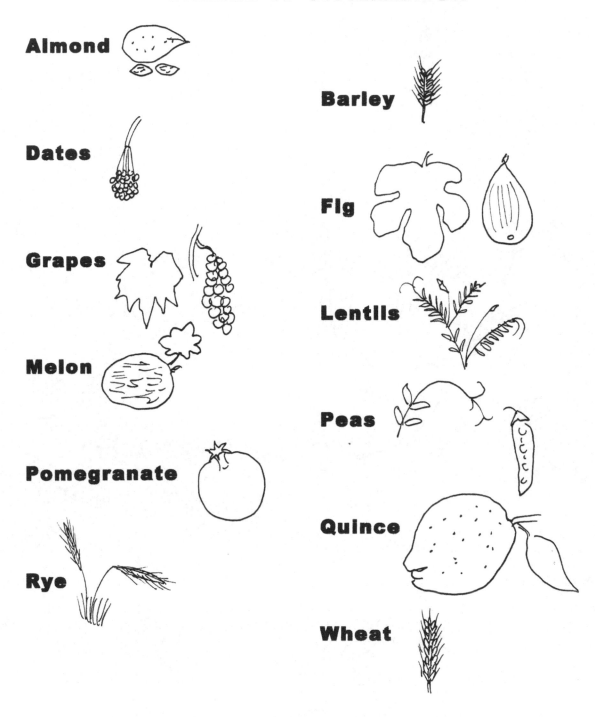

Almond

Barley

Dates

Fig

Grapes

Lentils

Melon

Peas

Pomegranate

Quince

Rye

Wheat

CENTER OF DIVERSITY
CULTIVATED PLANTS OF THE MIDDLE SEA

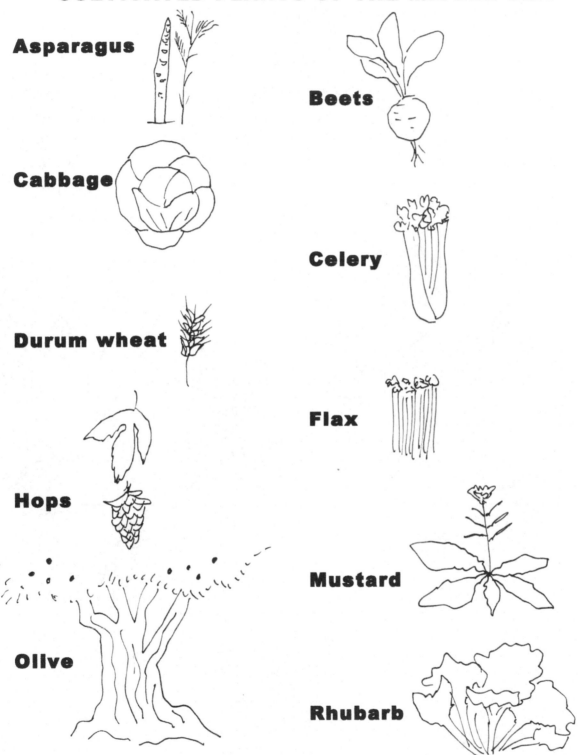

Asparagus

Beets

Cabbage

Celery

Durum wheat

Flax

Hops

Mustard

Olive

Rhubarb

32

CENTER OF DIVERSITY
CULTIVATED PLANTS FROM THE
GATEWAY OF EMPIRES

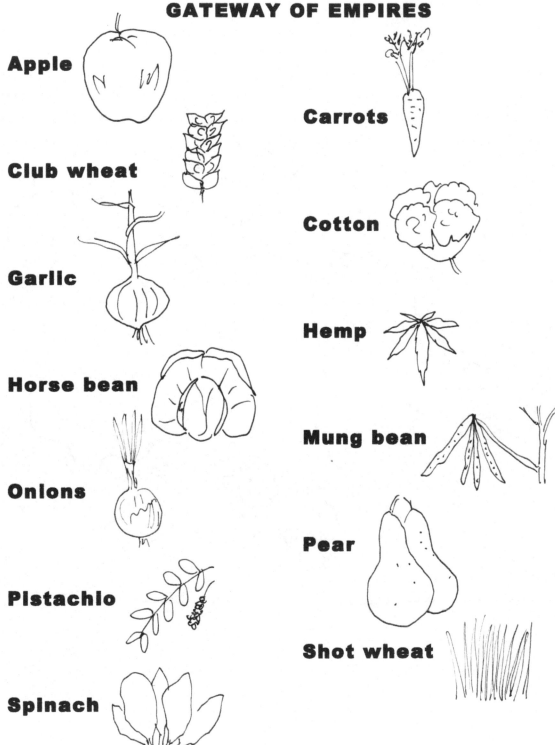

Apple

Club wheat

Garlic

Horse bean

Onions

Pistachio

Spinach

Carrots

Cotton

Hemp

Mung bean

Pear

Shot wheat

33

34

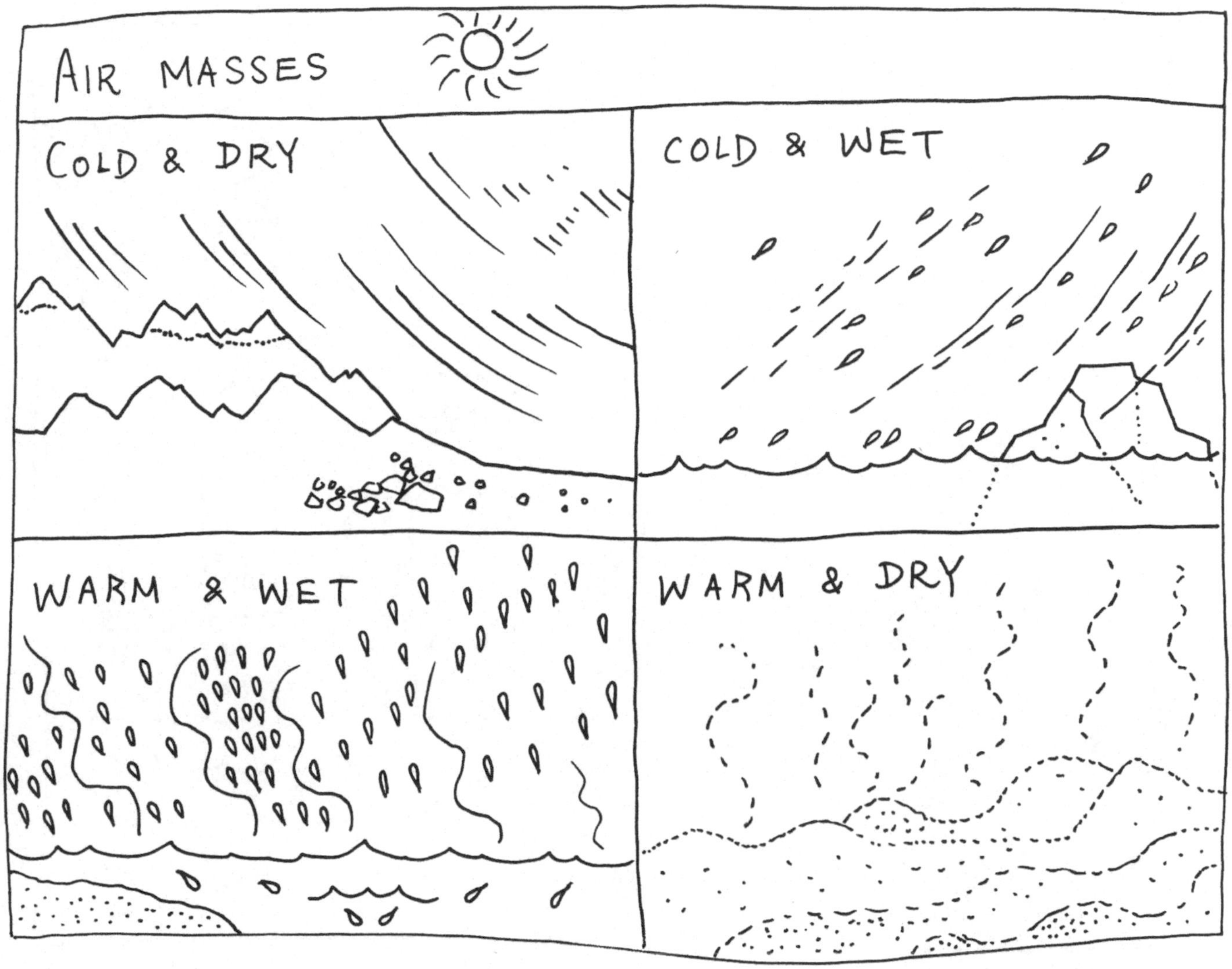

AIR MASSES

COLD & DRY

COLD & WET

WARM & WET

WARM & DRY

35

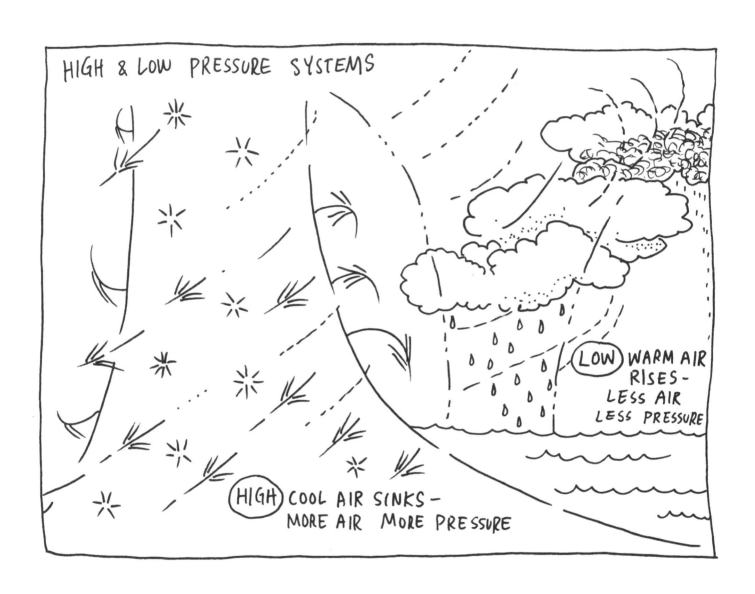

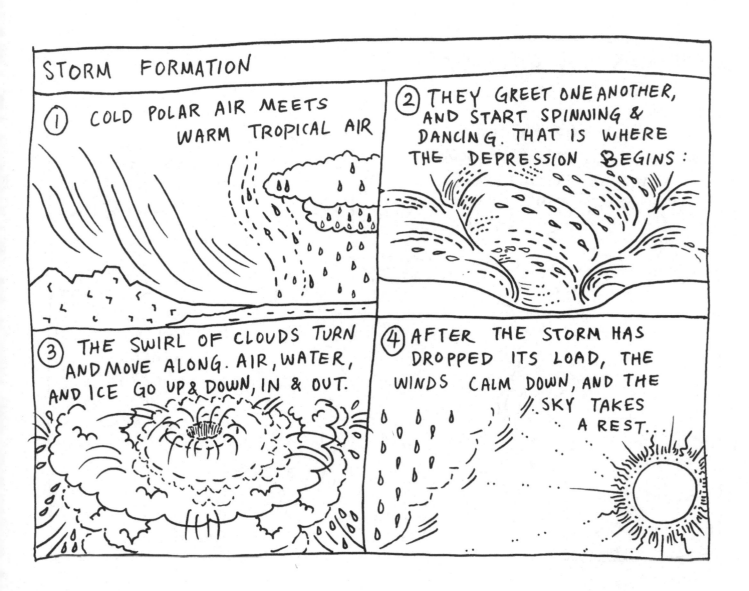

STORM FORMATION

1. COLD POLAR AIR MEETS WARM TROPICAL AIR

2. THEY GREET ONE ANOTHER, AND START SPINNING & DANCING. THAT IS WHERE THE DEPRESSION BEGINS:

3. THE SWIRL OF CLOUDS TURN AND MOVE ALONG. AIR, WATER, AND ICE GO UP & DOWN, IN & OUT.

4. AFTER THE STORM HAS DROPPED ITS LOAD, THE WINDS CALM DOWN, AND THE SKY TAKES A REST...

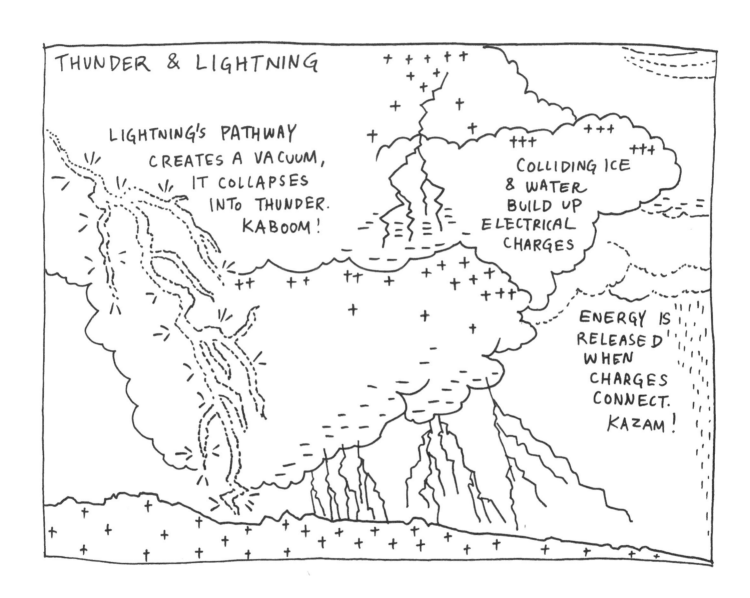

38

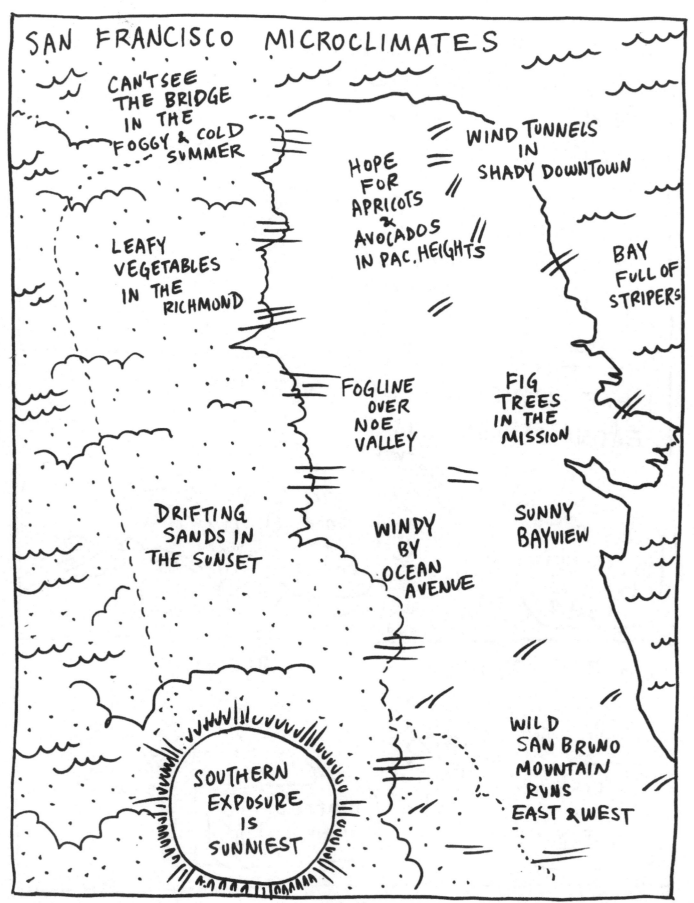

SIGNS OF WARMING TRENDS IN SF

Check the leaves:

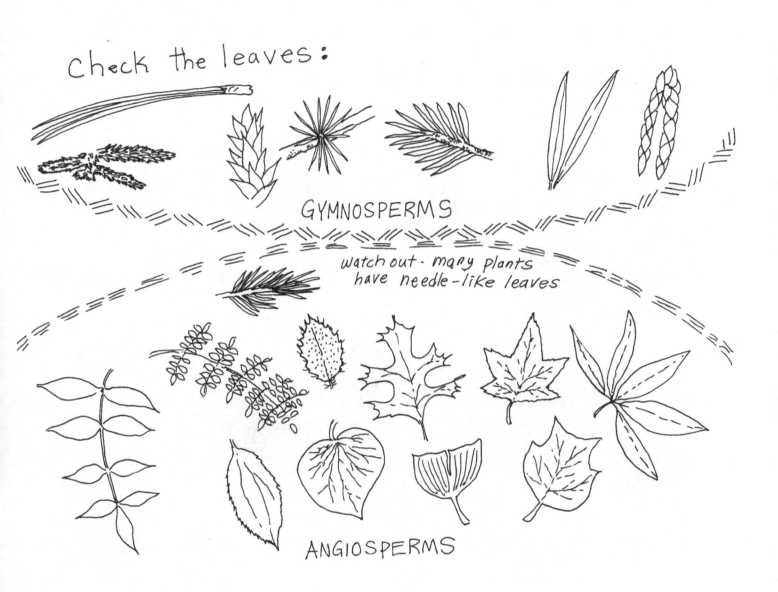

GYMNOSPERMS

watch out - many plants
have needle-like leaves

ANGIOSPERMS

43

Not all conifers have a 'cone'.

Arborvitae

Incense Cedar

Doug fir

redwood

Cedar

Cypress

Spruce

Pine

Podocarpus

Flavor the gin.

Juniper

From the Southern hemisphere

Berry-like cones

Yew

The seed is poison

Fir

Araucaria

MONOECIOUS CONIFERS : MALE POLLEN CONES &
FEMALE SEED CONES
TOGETHER ON THE SAME TREE
'ONE HOUSEHOLD'

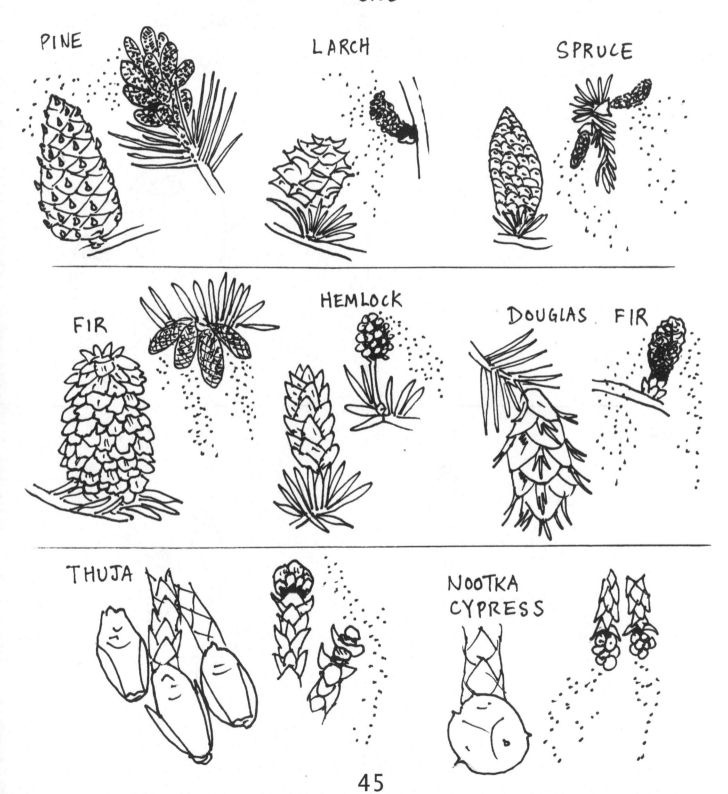

PINE

LARCH

SPRUCE

FIR

HEMLOCK

DOUGLAS FIR

THUJA

NOOTKA
CYPRESS

DIOECIOUS CONIFERS: FEMALE SEED CONES
ON ONE TREE.
MALE POLLEN CONES
ON ANOTHER TREE.
SEPARATED INTO TWO 'HOUSES'

JUNIPER FEMALE

YEW FEMALE

JUNIPER MALE

YEW MALE

46

Pine tree reproduction

Pollen grain touches the ovule.

outer skin of ovule

ovule

Pollen enters the female cone.

Pollen floats out of the male cones. The wind blows.

A gamete is formed from the cells of the male & female. The ovule grows into a seed. It sits at the base of the cone scale.

Male sperm cell meets the female egg cell.

Fertilization!!

Pollen grain releases the male sex cells. They grow a tube into the ovule.

Pine baby seedlings sprout up in the warm sun.

Finally, seed cone opens. Out fly the seeds! whirl to earth.

Female cones grow slowly. It takes a year or two to mature.

Fruits of some trees:

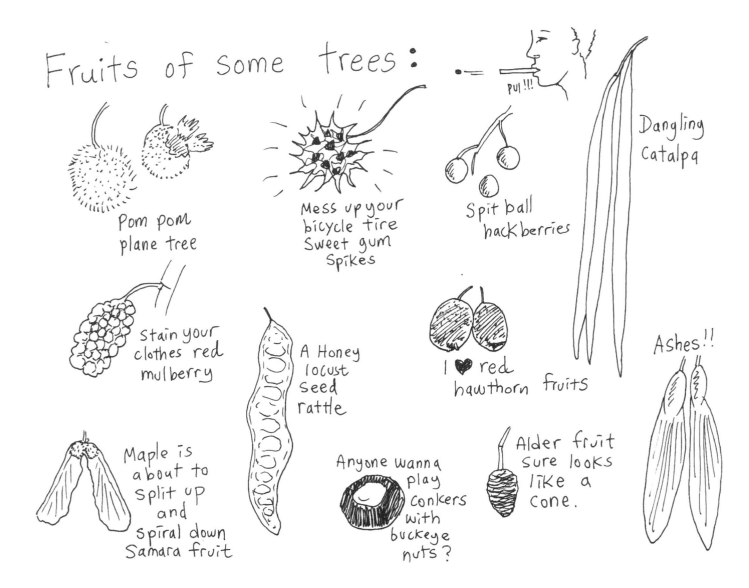

PUI !!!

Pom pom
plane tree

Mess up your
bicycle tire
Sweet gum
Spikes

Spit ball
hackberries

Dangling
Catalpa

Stain your
clothes red
mulberry

A Honey
locust
seed
rattle

I ♥ red
hawthorn fruits

Ashes!!

Maple is
about to
split up
and
spiral down
Samara fruit

Anyone wanna
play
conkers
with
buckeye
nuts?

Alder fruit
sure looks
like a
cone.

48

A few more tree fruits:

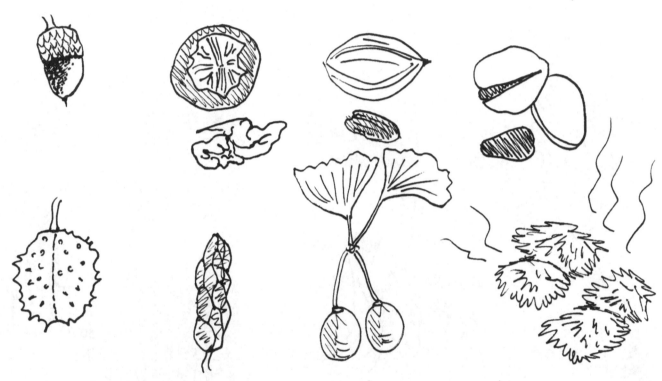

Find: Stinky ginkgo, brainy walnut, poky horse chestnut, light-it-up smoke bush, grind 'n leech acorn, green fleshed seed pistachio, P-P-P-P-P-Pe-Pecan, bunch-o-carpels magnolia.

Memorable barks

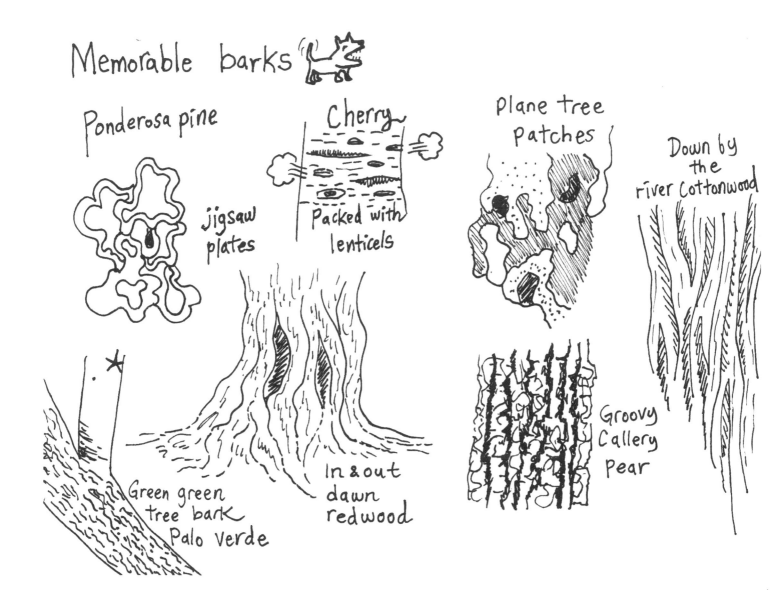

Ponderosa pine

jigsaw plates

Cherry

Packed with lenticels

Plane tree Patches

Down by the river Cottonwood

Green green tree bark Palo verde

In & out dawn redwood

Groovy Callery Pear

All in the Genus **Ficus**

— Five species of figs :

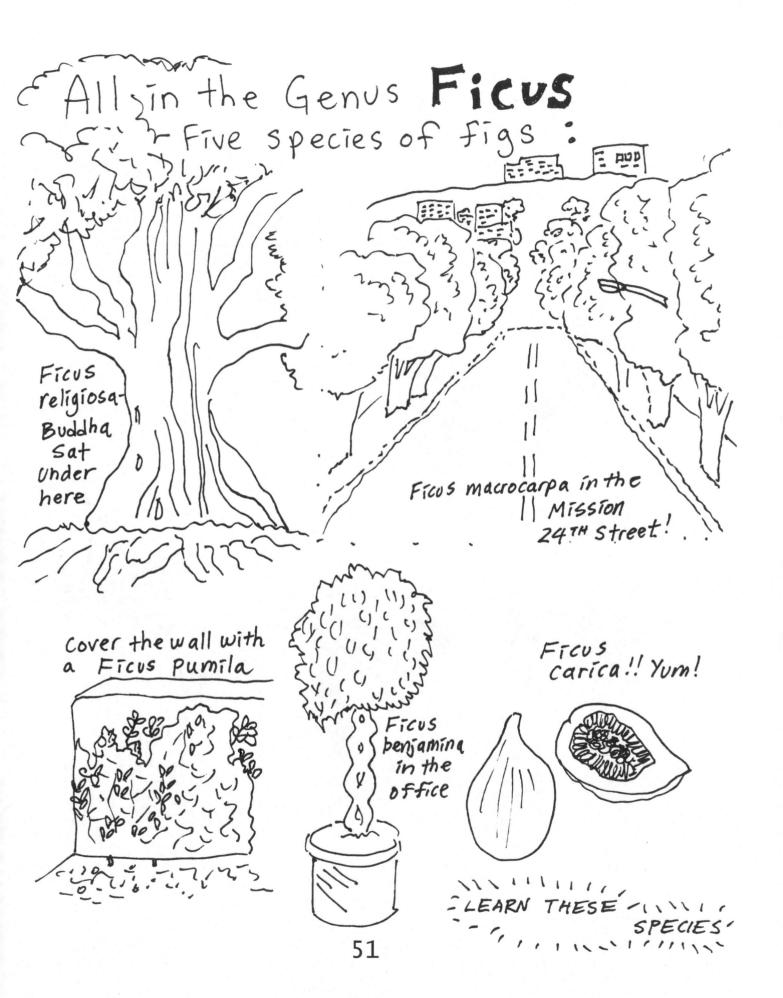

Ficus religiosa - Buddha Sat Under here

Ficus macrocarpa in the Mission 24th street!

Cover the wall with a Ficus Pumila

Ficus benjamina in the office

Ficus carica!! Yum!

LEARN THESE SPECIES

TUBES !!!

Vessels

Huge, wide tubes with plates ⬭ Pits ⦂⦂ and Perforations ▶▶

Plate Variations

Plates with pores

Porous membranes connect cells

Excellent sap flow in broadleaf trees with vessels.

Tracheids

Large diameter thin walled 'Spring wood'

Small diameter thick walled dark 'Summer Wood'

Easy to see growth rings in conifers with tracheids

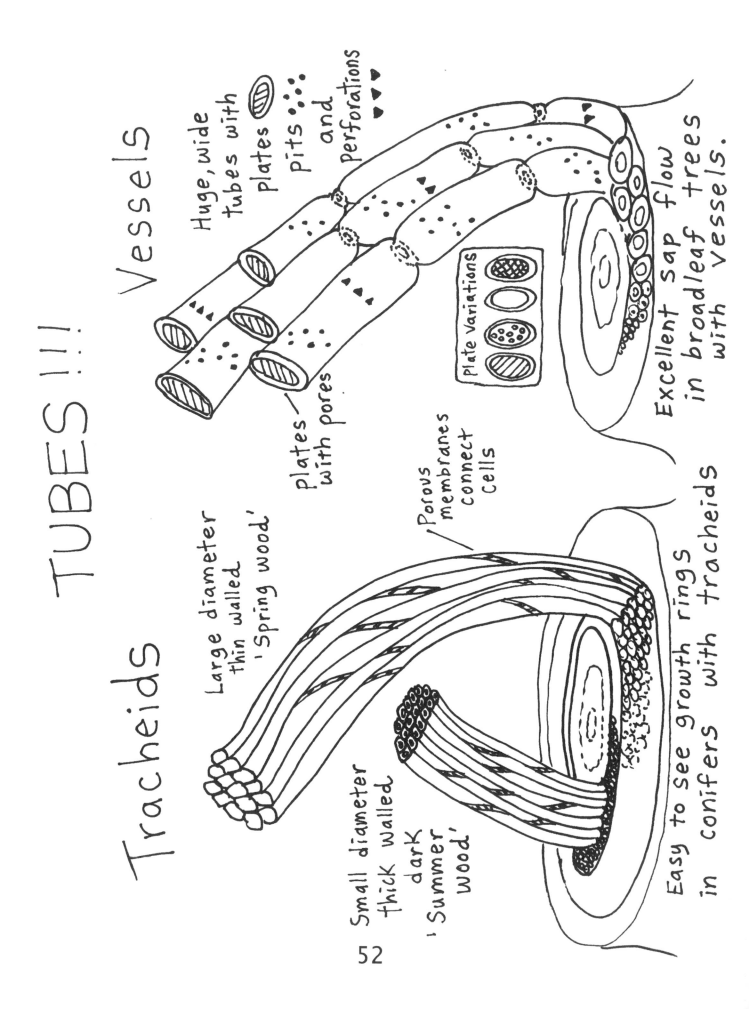

52

Why two plant species don't mate in nature:

How two plant species mate and create hybrids

Why can't a plant mate with itself? (Self-infertile)

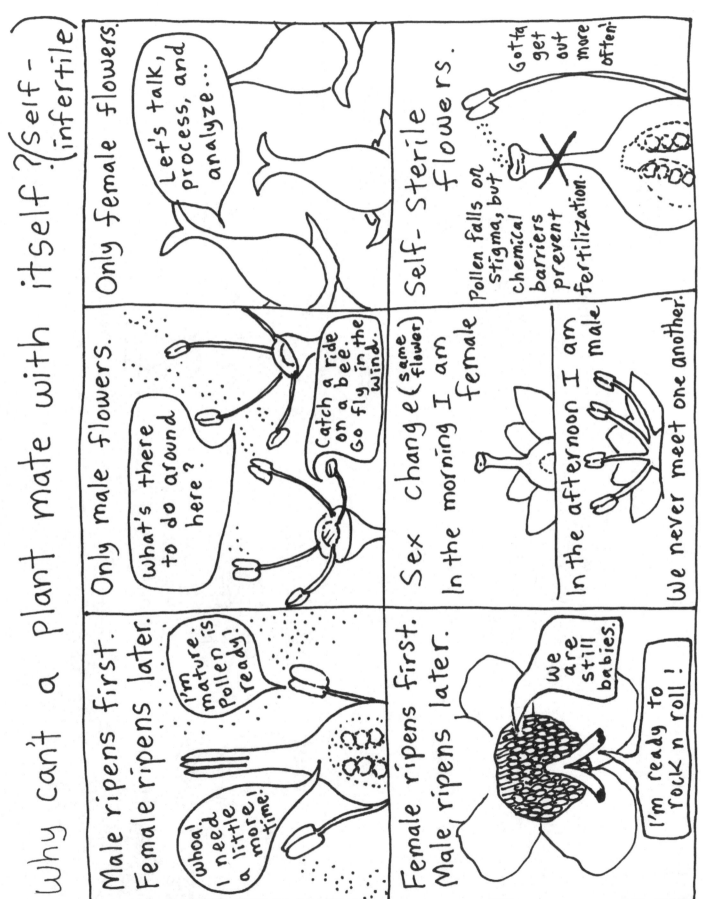

What plant is self-fertile?
What plant can mate with itself and have babies?

Angiosperm pollination: Double Fertilization

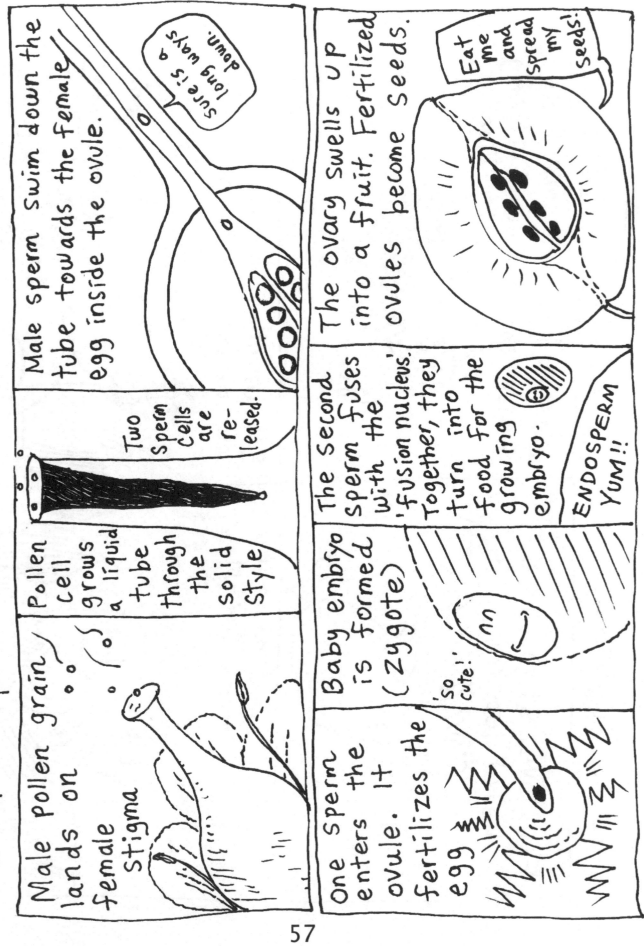

Male pollen grain lands on female stigma

Pollen cell grows a liquid tube through the solid style

Male sperm swim down the tube towards the female egg inside the ovule.

Two sperm cells are released.

"Sure's a long ways down."

One sperm enters the ovule. It fertilizes the egg

The second sperm fuses with the 'fusion nucleus.' Together, they turn into food for the growing embryo.

The ovary swells up into a fruit. Fertilized ovules become seeds.

Baby embryo is formed (zygote)

"so cute!"

ENDOSPERM YUM!!

"Eat me and spread my seeds!"

Cardiac glycoside

Foxglove stimulates heart contractions

Milkweed poisons are stored inside the Monarch butterfly Caterpillar

Lily of the valley spring from Mary's tears

Strophanthus is used as arrow poison in Africa

Anthaquinone Glycosides

Cascara Sagrada helps you release stools

whew! Holy bark!

A purge using Senna can be violent & too strong

Bloody poop

Aloe Vera is a Purgative, cleans out poison, parasite & poop. It is also useful for burns & skin irritation

Goopy!

Take too much laxatives and you won't be able to poop without them.

stuck again?!

How about a plate of fiber instead? Fresh greens & lentils!

Glycoside - Saponins

Ceanothus flowers and water make a nice lather-soap.

Buckeye nuts poison fish in a dammed up stream. The Saponins destroy the red blood cells and release the hemoglobin.

Soapbark Quillaja is good buddies with Chilean wine Palm

Beans, tomatoes, spinach - all have Saponins.

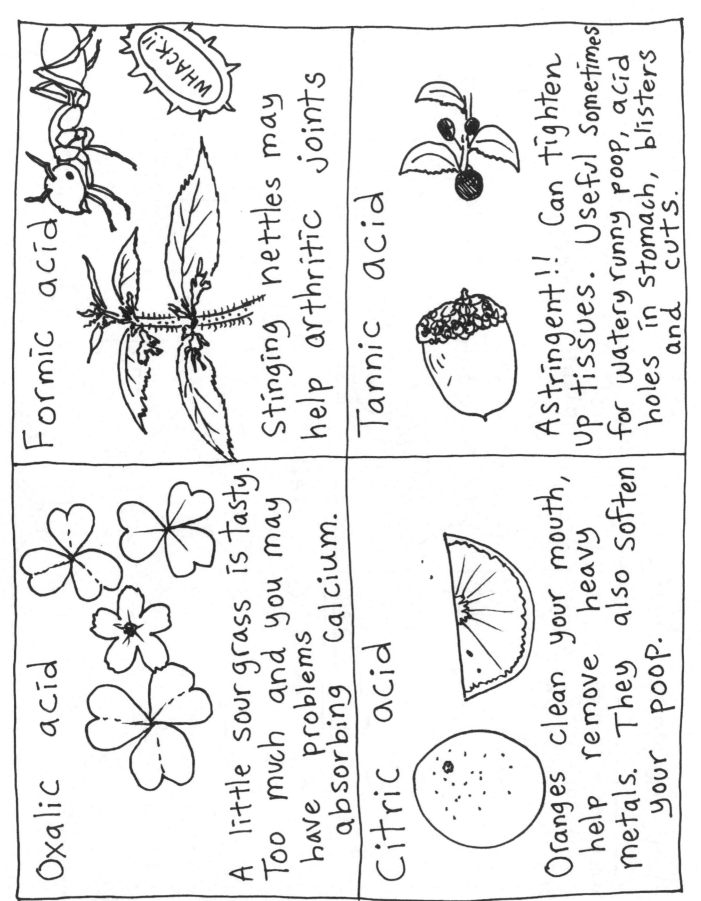

Formic acid

WHACK!!

Stinging nettles may help arthritic joints

Oxalic acid

A little sour grass is tasty. Too much and you may have problems absorbing calcium.

Tannic acid

Astringent!! Can tighten up tissues. Useful sometimes for watery runny poop, acid holes in stomach, blisters and cuts.

Citric acid

Oranges clean your mouth, help remove heavy metals. They also soften your poop.

61

Plant hormone : Abscisic acid

62

Soil profile:

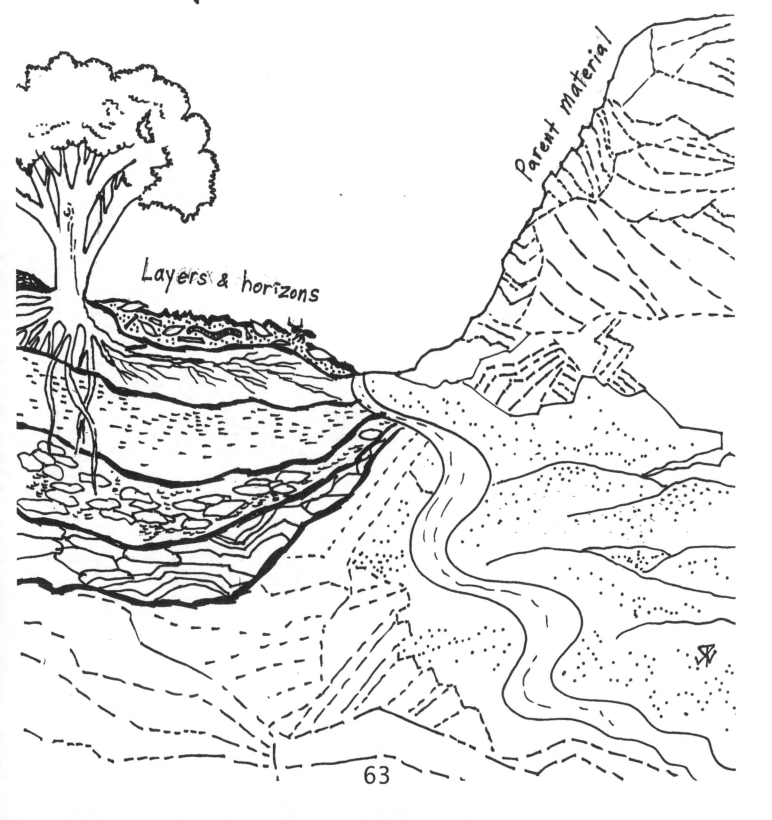

Parent material

Layers & horizons

Percolation: water moving in the soil

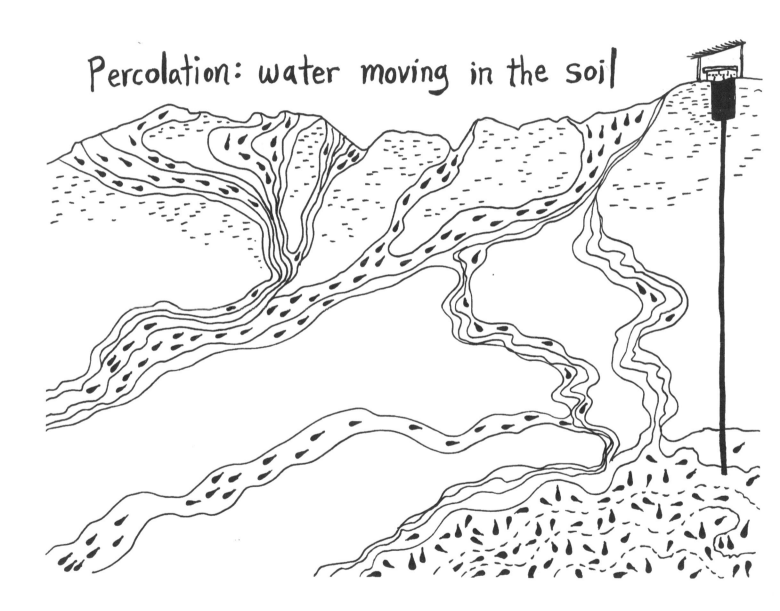

Soil is a sponge
Soil is a filter

Soil is filled
with life

Soil holds up
roads & foundations

Soil eats
the dead

Soil & plants are B.F.F. BEST FRIENDS FOREVER

Soil action & drama ①

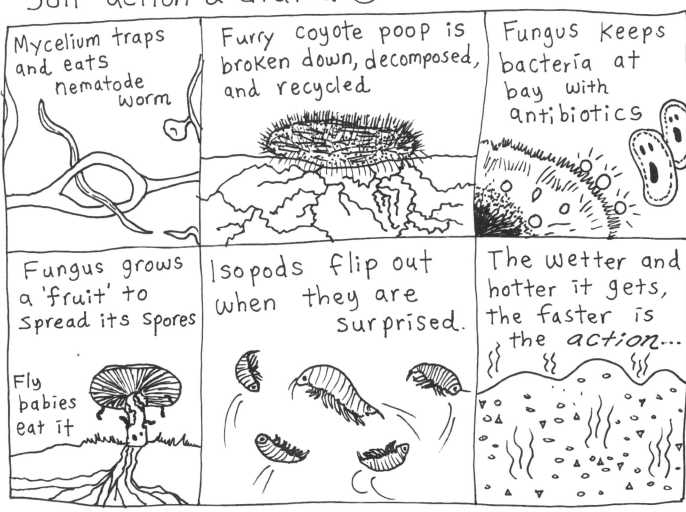

Mycelium traps and eats nematode worm

Furry coyote poop is broken down, decomposed, and recycled

Fungus keeps bacteria at bay with antibiotics

Fungus grows a 'fruit' to spread its spores

Fly babies eat it

Isopods flip out when they are surprised.

The wetter and hotter it gets, the faster is the *action*...

Soil action & drama ②

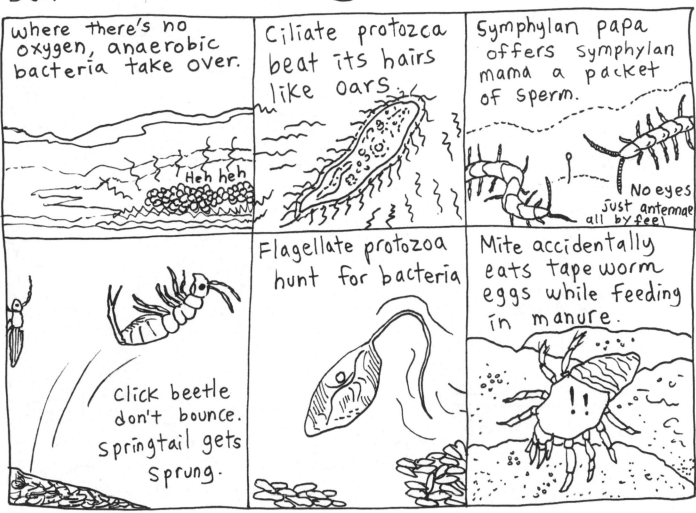

where there's no oxygen, anaerobic bacteria take over.

Heh heh

Ciliate protozoa beat its hairs like oars.

Symphylan papa offers symphylan mama a packet of sperm.

No eyes just antennae all by feel

Click beetle don't bounce. Springtail gets sprung.

Flagellate protozoa hunt for bacteria

Mite accidentally eats tapeworm eggs while feeding in manure.

!!

Cover Crop

Plant some fava beans or clover

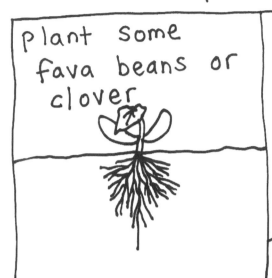

Fava says "HOMES FOR BACTERIA! HOMES FOR BACTERIA! ONLY *RHIZOBIUM* NEED APPLY!"

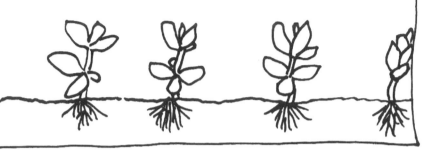

Rhizobium in the soil moves in, settles on the roots.

Rhizobium grabs nitrogen in the air and converts it to soil nitrogen. Gives it to the fava bean.

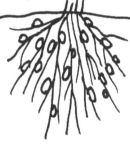

Thank you friend. I will use nitrogen for green growth.

No problems! Thanks for the place to live

UNDERGROUND SYMBIOSIS

Compost ① Raisin' soil pets

My best friends are fungus & bacteria

I feed them grass clippings, kitchen waste, fallen leaves, and branches.

All they ask for is air and water. Basic needs. Then, they eat, get hot, and reproduce all day and all night long.

Compost ② : Fungus & bacteria food

Soil pets are happiest with a mix of materials to eat_ about half-green nitrogen-rich materials, half-brown carbon-rich matter. Pile 'em up in the compost!

Nitrogen goes into making amino acids, proteins and alkaloids

Carbon goes into making sugars, starches, cellulose, fats, and alcohols

The approximate ratio in live organisms is 30 carbon atoms to 1 nitrogen atom.

Potting soils ①: Materials & proportions

'Generic' mix: Make sure mix holds water & has air pockets. Don't let it get goopy. or dry out.

Bonsai mix: some sand and grit, a pinch of compost and a spoon of baked clay

Cactus & succulents from the desert Mostly well drained materials. Pumice and sand. A little bark or coir fiber.

Orchids that grow in crotches of trees All bark! Fertilize time to time.

Potting Soils ② Ingredients

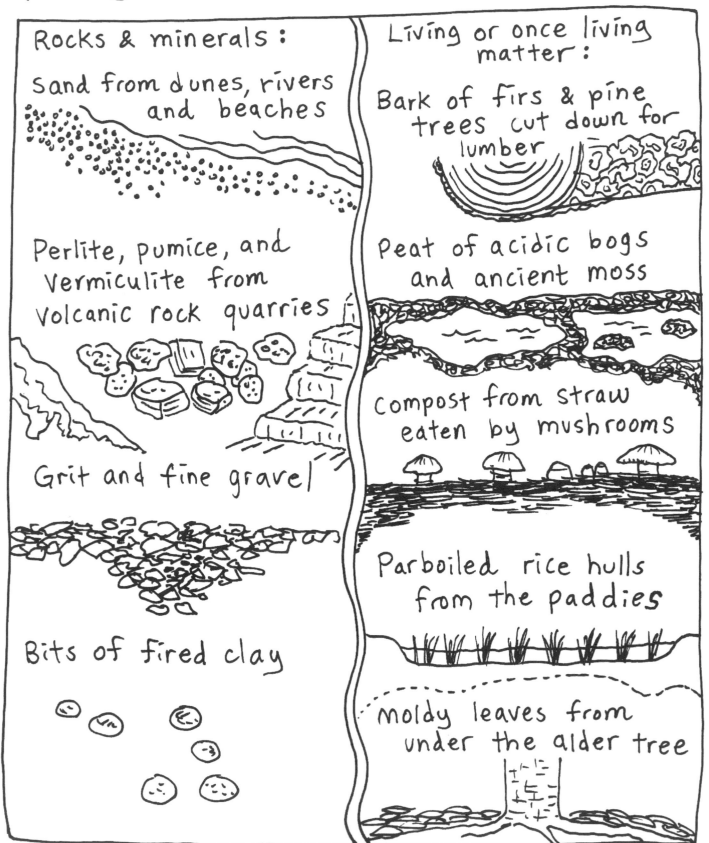

Rocks & minerals:

Sand from dunes, rivers and beaches

Perlite, pumice, and vermiculite from volcanic rock quarries

Grit and fine gravel

Bits of fired clay

Living or once living matter:

Bark of firs & pine trees cut down for lumber

Peat of acidic bogs and ancient moss

Compost from straw eaten by mushrooms

Parboiled rice hulls from the paddies

Moldy leaves from under the alder tree

'Poor' soils are okay!! Just find the right plant

Soil action & drama ③

Panel 1: Soil engineers burrow in mucus tunnels

Panel 2: Millipede eats its own shed skeleton

Panel 3: undertakers scavenge the dead

Panel 4: Slug gnaws off its own penis when it is stuck

Panel 5: The water bear is pretty much IMMORTAL

Panel 6: A handful of dirt is the home of many many organisms

SOIL LOVE

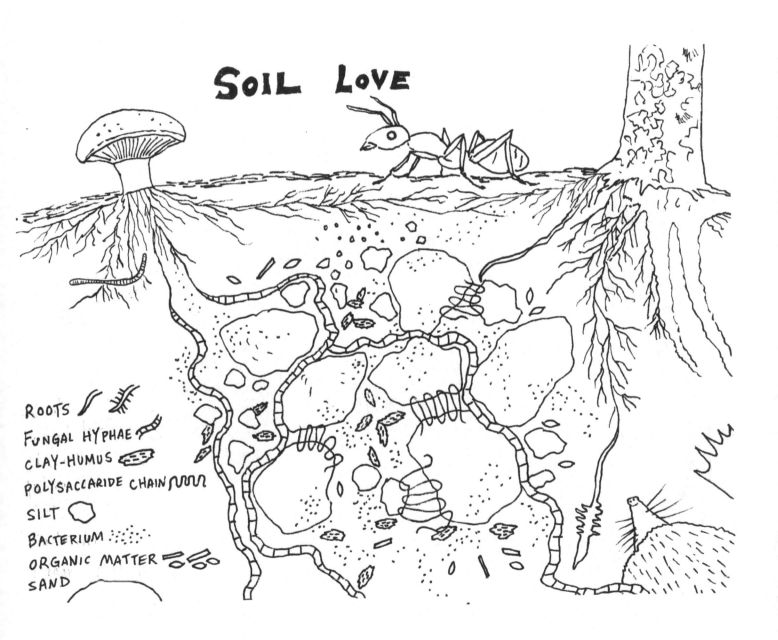

ROOTS
FUNGAL HYPHAE
CLAY-HUMUS
POLYSACCARIDE CHAIN
SILT
BACTERIUM
ORGANIC MATTER
SAND

DUST BOWL

Floods, wind, time and weathering makes topsoil.

Topsoil is stuck together in aggregates of humus and clay. Bacteria and fungus compete for some organic matter to eat.

Humus can sit around for thousands of years. Soil grows deep & rich. Fertility!

Cultivation of the soil breaks the ancient soil bonds. Oxygen and microbes eat the life- poo- goop- colloids.

Soil structure is destroyed. Its ability to hold water & nutrients is decreased.

Here comes the drought. Then come the wind storms. All the little dry soil particles fly away. Bye bye topsoil !!

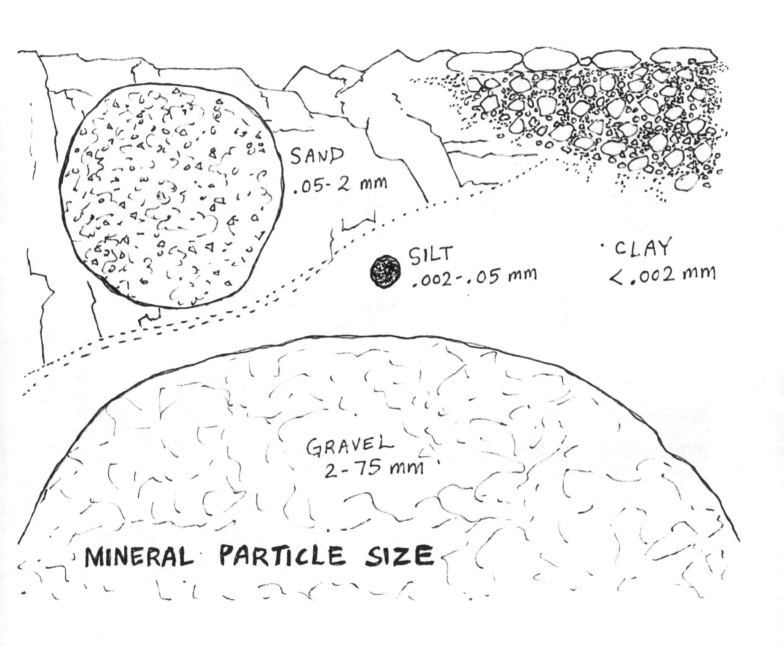

SAND
.05- 2 mm

SILT
.002-.05 mm

CLAY
< .002 mm

GRAVEL
2- 75 mm

MINERAL PARTICLE SIZE

BEAUTIFUL CLAY

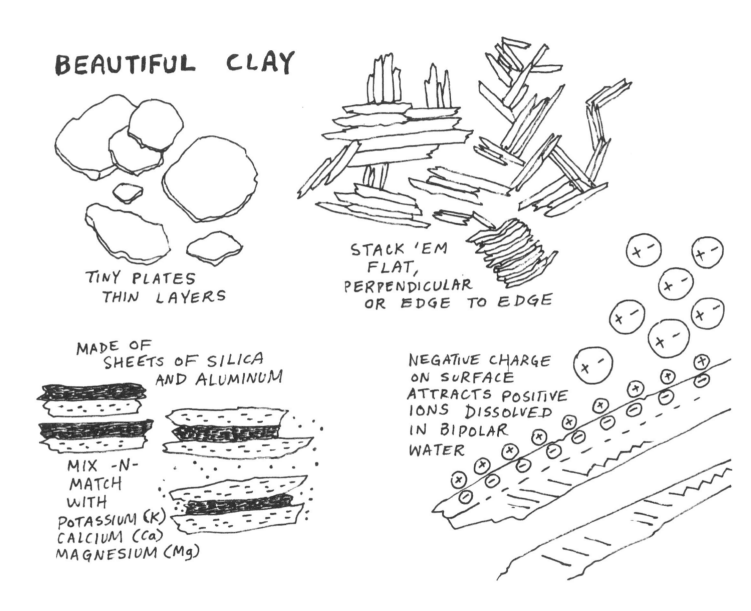

TINY PLATES
THIN LAYERS

STACK 'EM
FLAT,
PERPENDICULAR
OR EDGE TO EDGE

MADE OF
SHEETS OF SILICA
AND ALUMINUM

MIX -N-
MATCH
WITH
POTASSIUM (K)
CALCIUM (Ca)
MAGNESIUM (Mg)

NEGATIVE CHARGE
ON SURFACE
ATTRACTS POSITIVE
IONS DISSOLVED
IN BIPOLAR
WATER

SOIL CONSISTENCE & STRENGTH
(AT THE BEACH)

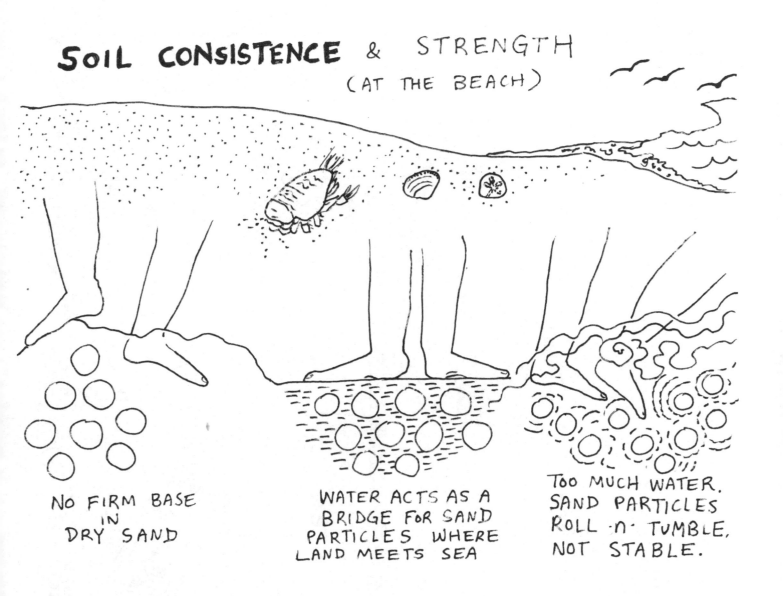

NO FIRM BASE IN DRY SAND

WATER ACTS AS A BRIDGE FOR SAND PARTICLES WHERE LAND MEETS SEA

TOO MUCH WATER. SAND PARTICLES ROLL ·n· TUMBLE, NOT STABLE.

Colloids of clay and humus : Properties

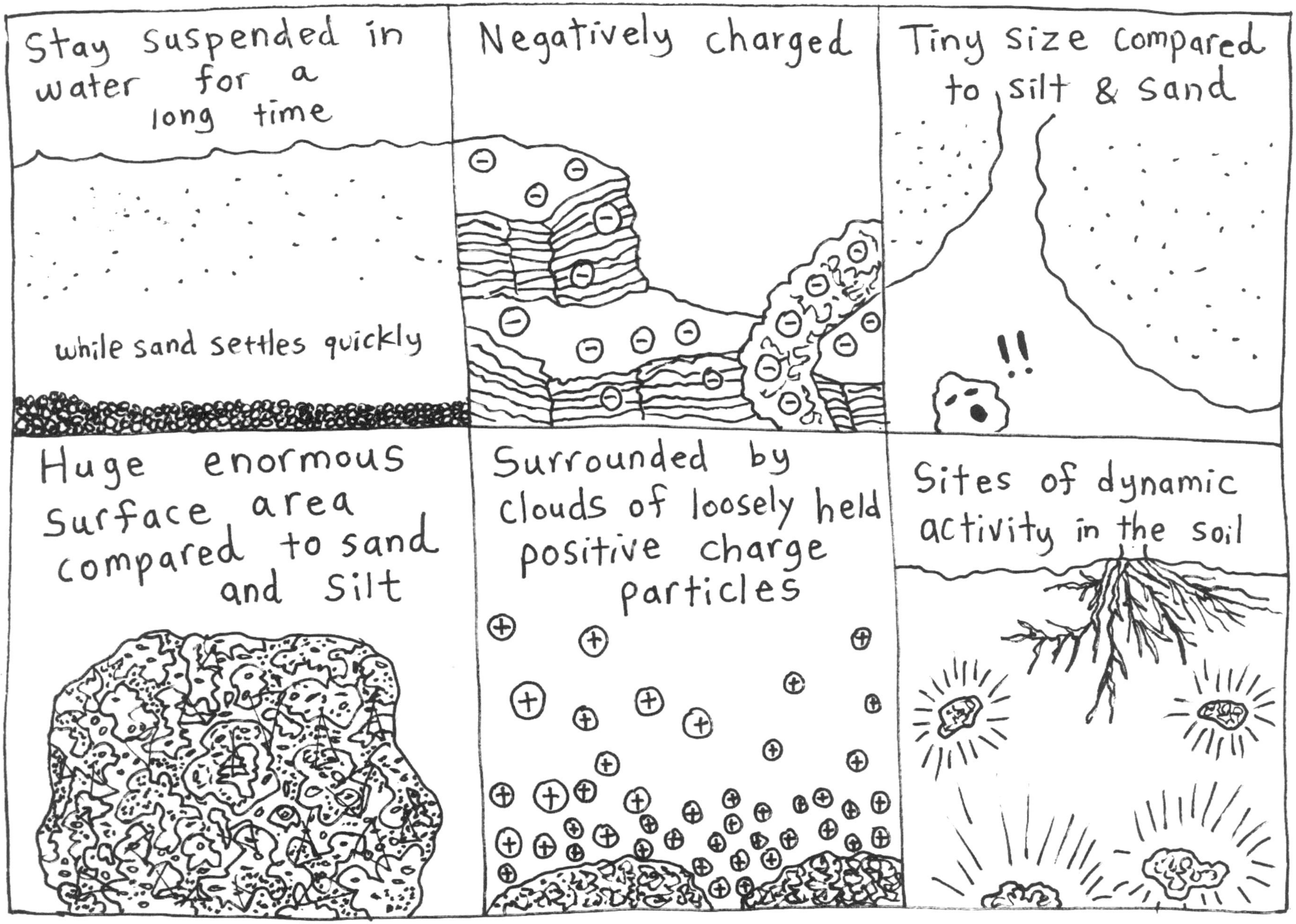

Stay suspended in water for a long time	Negatively charged	Tiny size compared to silt & sand
while sand settles quickly		
Huge enormous surface area compared to sand and silt	Surrounded by clouds of loosely held positive charge particles	Sites of dynamic activity in the soil

Structure of clay & humus

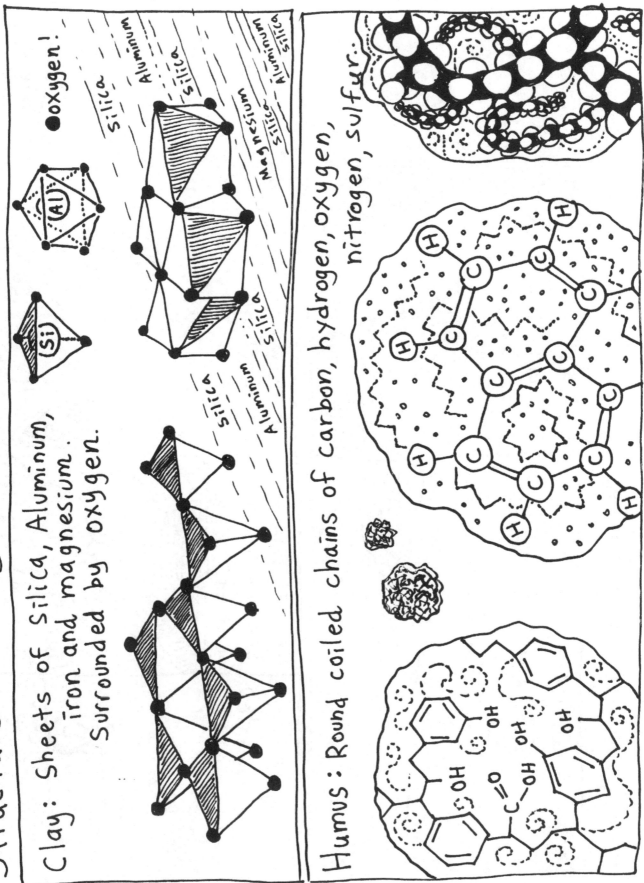

Clay: Sheets of silica, Aluminum, iron and magnesium. Surrounded by oxygen.

●oxygen!

(Al)

(Si)

silica
Aluminum
silica
Magnesium
silica
Aluminum
silica

silica
Aluminum
silica

Humus: Round coiled chains of carbon, hydrogen, oxygen, nitrogen, sulfur.

Soil problem - Salinity

Anions⊖ and positively charged sites ⊕

Bonds at Cation exchange sites:

If numbers of ions are equal »»»»

Nothin' quite like a hydrogen bond!

yeah, I'm jealous. when you gonna give up your spot?

What are you lookin' at? I just got here

But, the negative charges are so attractive

I weigh more

Just cause your atomic mass is bigger I gotta float here?

Ahh. Finally. A spot. Scram Potassium! My valence is +2 !!

I don't care if you lose two electrons! I'm patient.

Somehow I don't think I'm gonna stay here for long...

If only bacteria could change me into a negative nitrate ion...

Well, at least my bond is stronger than Sodium's.

That is just being mean.

Mass action: when a lot of ions overwhelm exchange sites

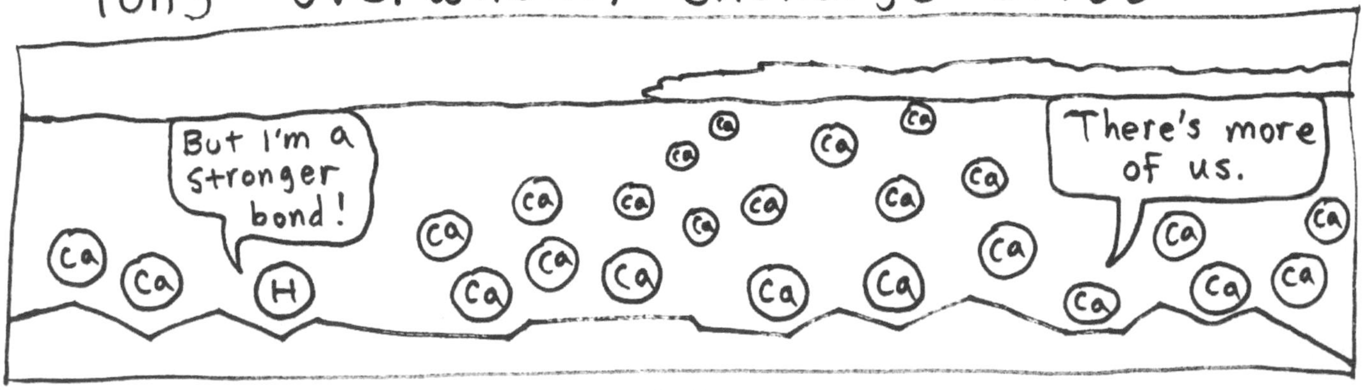

But I'm a stronger bond!

There's more of us.

Soil problem # 1
what is a fertility unit?

(a) Paleolithic goddess.

(b)

$$(\sqrt{age})\left(\frac{12}{weight}\right) +$$

(zinc intake per day in mg)^2

+ (Stress level per hour in pbp*)^2

+ (number of times you have seen a full moon)^2 = one fertility unit

* pbp is "panic button pressed"

(c) A set of quintuplets.

(d) Cation exchange capacity CEC

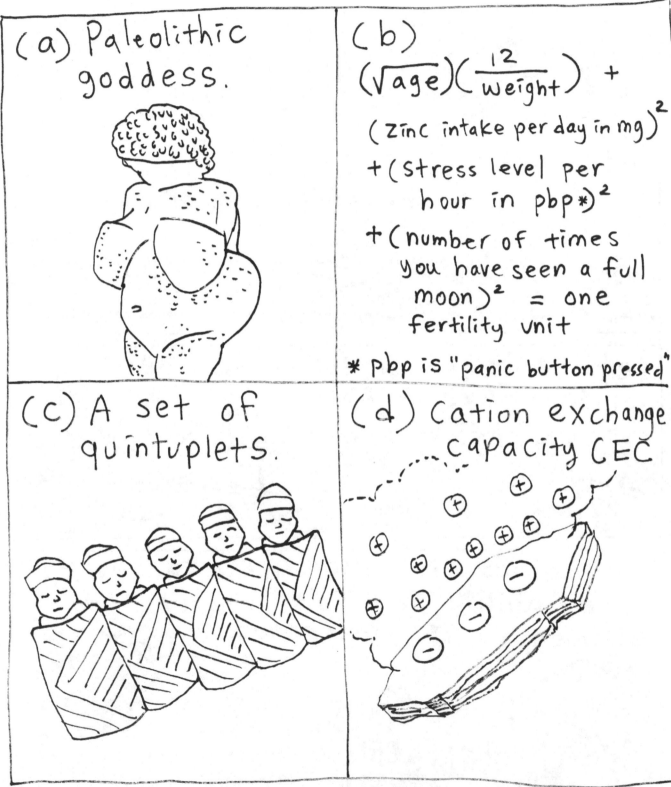

Soil is alive!

Start with mineral particles of sand, silt, or clays.

Add manures and compost, old leaves, and branches!

Let bacteria & fungi do their work. Feed & excrete, feed & excrete.

Soil binds together in sticky chunks. The ability to hold water and nutrients is increased.

Soil Pollutants

By the train tracks

Old paint with lead

"Hey it made the paint flow smoother!"

Arsenic in the lumber

Kept fungus from eating the wood

Mercury that caught bits of gold.

Get every little speck!

Metals are mined, concentrated, then return to the earth and sea.

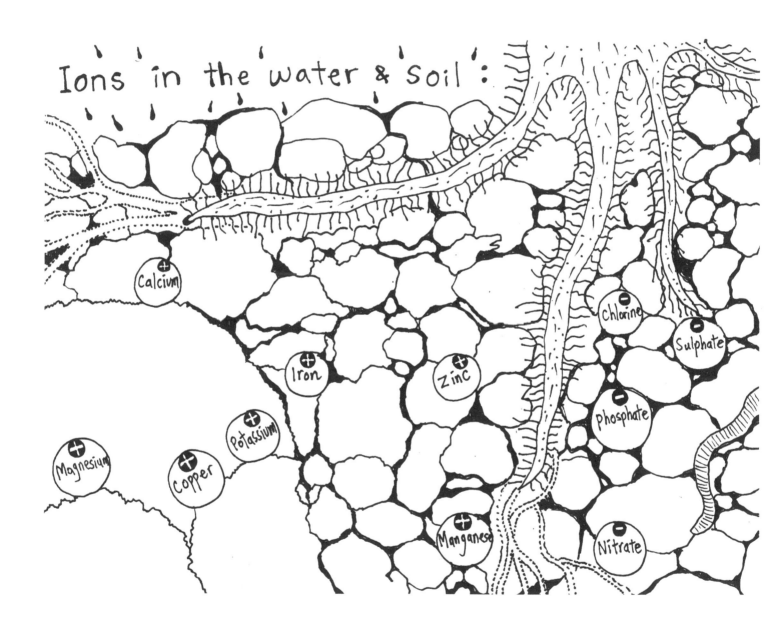

Ions are:

Docked on clay

Sloshin' in solution (water)

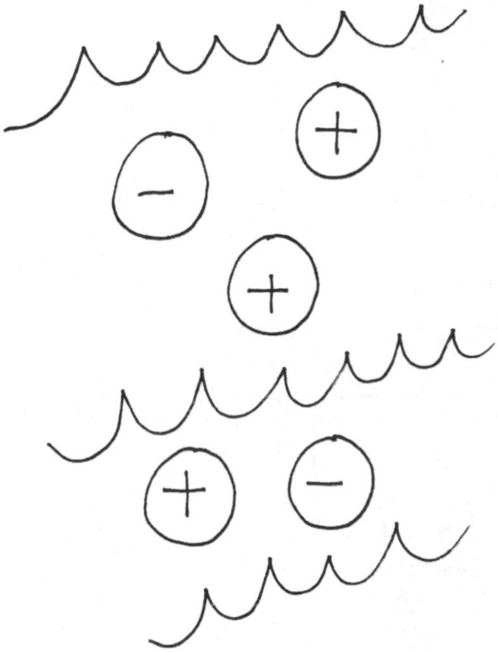

Bound to rock & carbon matter

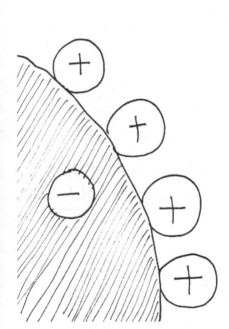

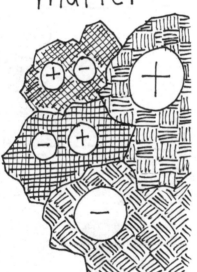

Inorganic fertilizers come in:

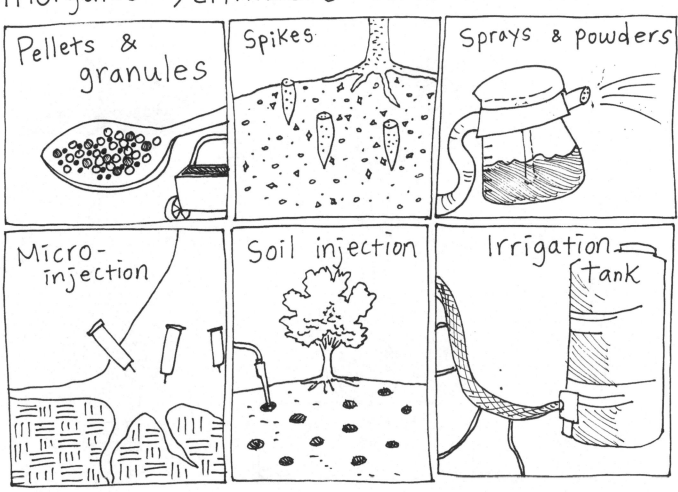

Pellets & granules

Spikes

Sprays & powders

Micro-injection

Soil injection

Irrigation tank

Organic fertilizers - Slow & steady

Compost

Manures

Guano

Blood & bone

Seaweed

Fava beans & clover

Gardeners & nitrogen ①

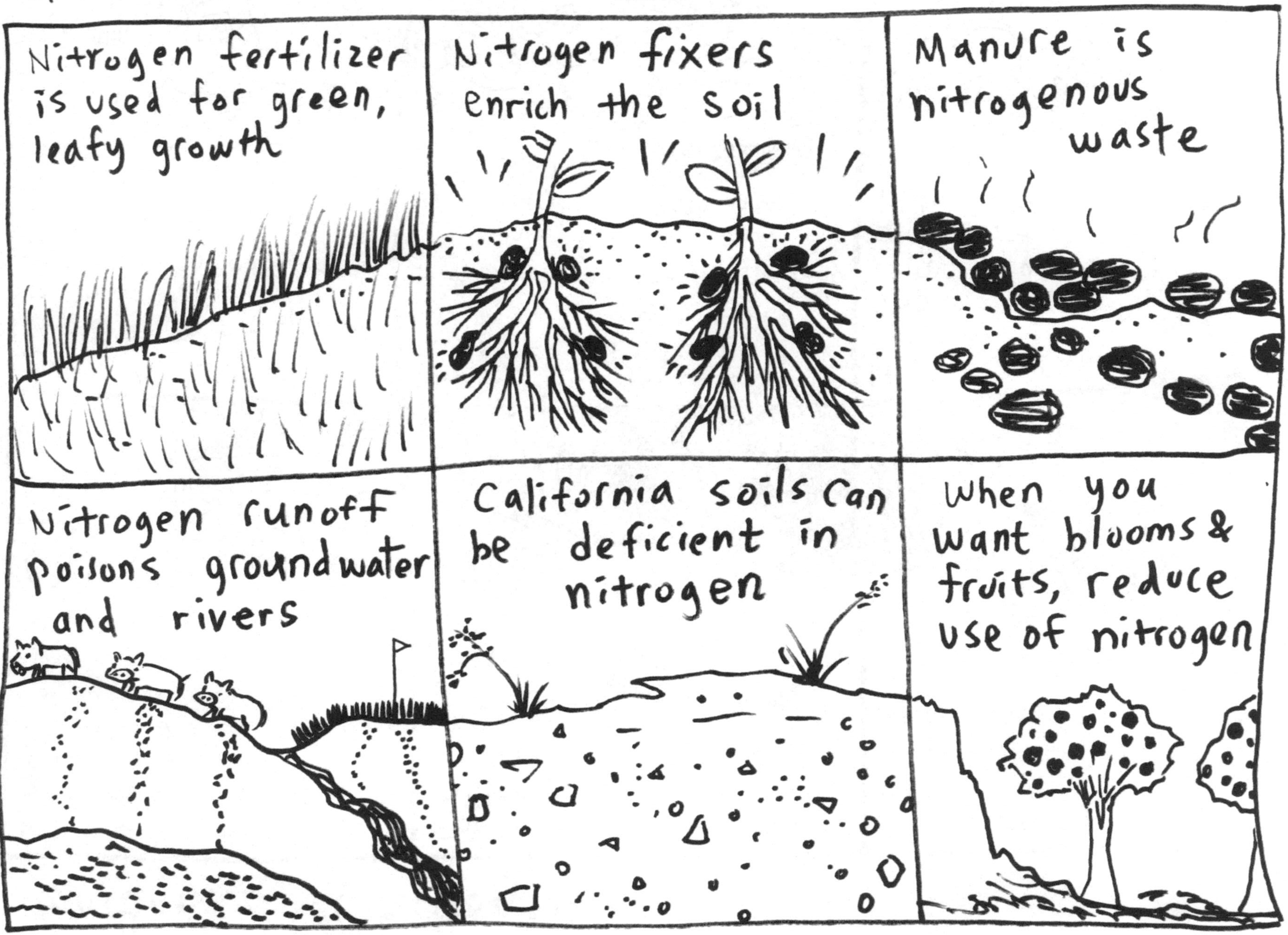

Nitrogen fertilizer is used for green, leafy growth

Nitrogen fixers enrich the soil

Manure is nitrogenous waste

Nitrogen runoff poisons groundwater and rivers

California soils can be deficient in nitrogen

When you want blooms & fruits, reduce use of nitrogen

Gardeners & nitrogen ②

When a plant breathes in nitrogen gas from the atmosphere, it can't use it for green growth. The gas is inert.

For plants to use the nitrogen, atmospheric nitrogen must become soil nitrogen. NITROGEN FIXATION

(N) (NN) (NN) (NN)

(H N H) (H N H) (H N H)

A lightning strike can move nitrogen in the air into the earth.

When a gardener breathes in nitrogen gas on land, there is no effect. The gas is inert.

When the gardener goes scuba diving dark & deep, nitrogen gas enters the body rapidly. The gardener goes dizzy and drunk with nitrogen narcosis.

If the gardener comes up to the surface too fast, nitrogen gas expands and bursts body parts.

Gardeners & nitrogen ③

Nitrogen is a part of every protein every amino acid

Rib eye

Quinoa

Nitrogen is a part of every alkaloid

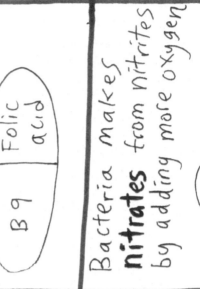
Caffeine

Codeine

Heroin
nicotine

Nitrogen is a part of every B vitamin

B2 Riboflavin

B9 | Folic acid

Bacteria makes **Ammonia** – by adding nitrogen gas and hydrogen

Bacteria makes **nitrites** from Ammonia, by adding oxygen and subtracting hydrogen

Bacteria makes **nitrates** from nitrites by adding more oxygen

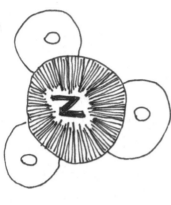

Gardeners & nitrogen ④

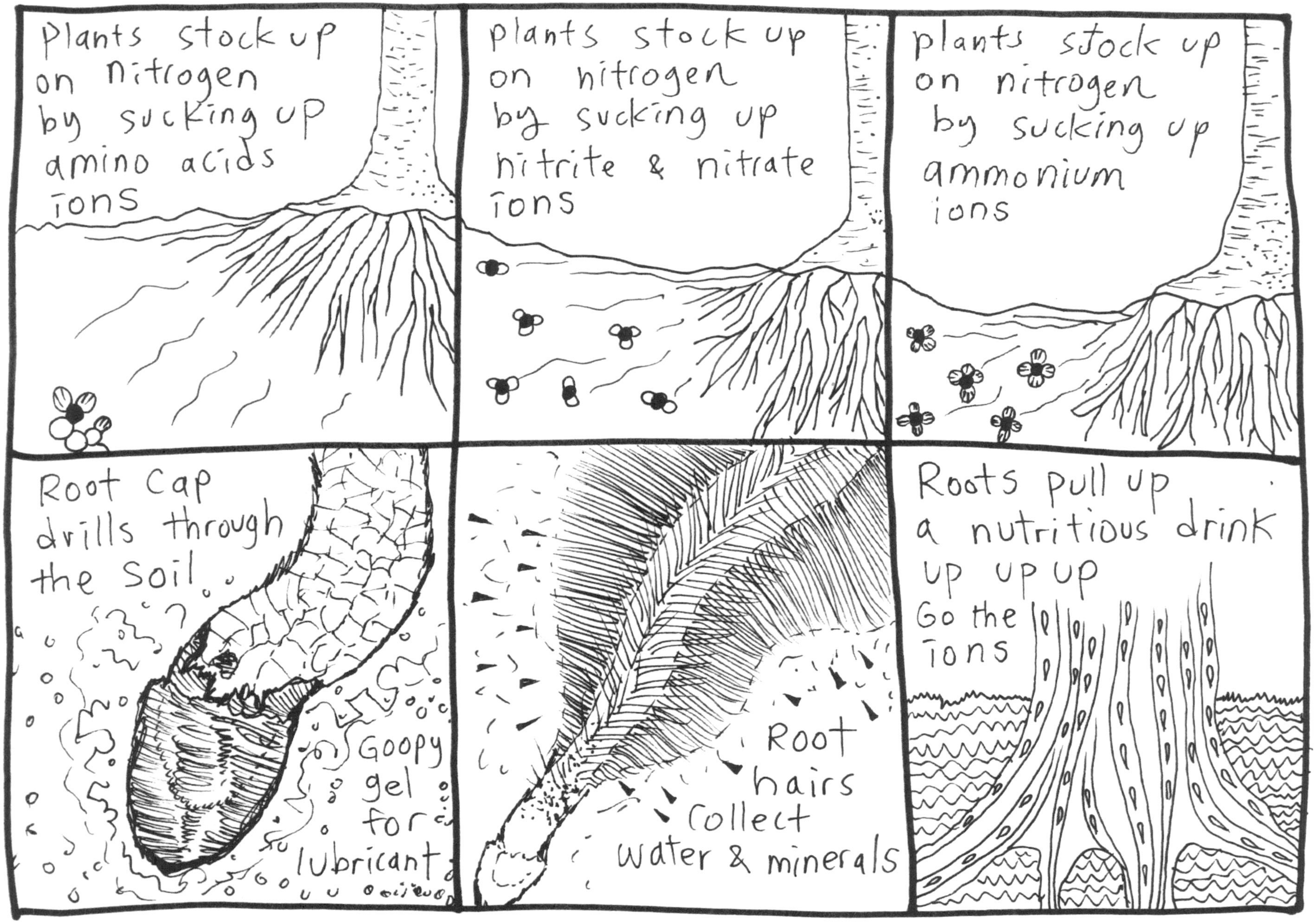

Plants stock up on nitrogen by sucking up amino acids ions

Plants stock up on nitrogen by sucking up nitrite & nitrate ions

Plants stock up on nitrogen by sucking up ammonium ions

Roots pull up a nutritious drink up up up Go the ions

Root hairs collect water & minerals

Root cap drills through the soil. Goopy gel for lubricant

Gardeners & nitrogen ⑤

Old time:
Manure
Blood, bone, hoofs, feathers

Natural:
Guano
Plants, animals, and rocks
Saltpetre mineral

Modern:
Ammonium nitrate
34.40% Nitrogen

Synthetic:
Calcium nitrate
15.5-0-0
50 LBS. NET WT.

Ammonium Sulfate
21-0-0
• CONTAINS SULFUR (24%)

Chemicals: made in a factory
UREA
NITROGEN: 46.0% BY
WEIGHT: 25 KG NE

Natural gas + Nitrogen gas + heat + pressure

SF TREES – SOIL-WATER RELATIONSHIPS

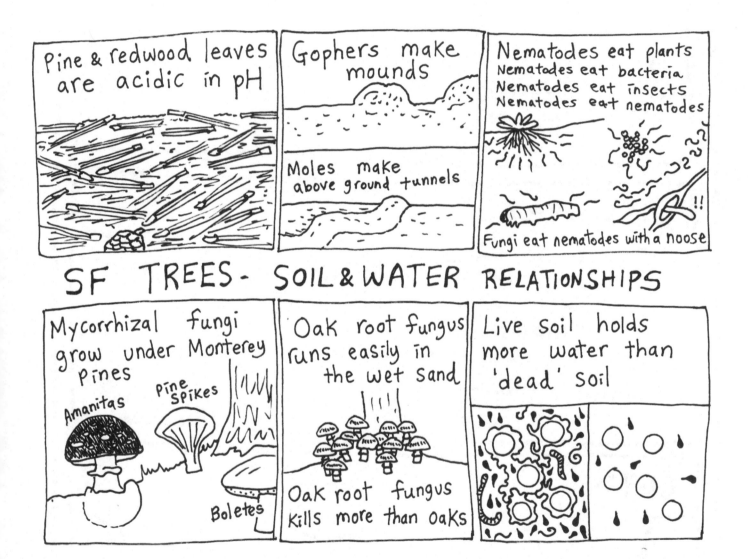

Pine & redwood leaves are acidic in pH

Gophers make mounds

Moles make above ground tunnels

Nematodes eat plants
Nematodes eat bacteria
Nematodes eat insects
Nematodes eat nematodes

Fungi eat nematodes with a noose

SF TREES - SOIL & WATER RELATIONSHIPS

Mycorrhizal fungi grow under Monterey pines

Amanitas   Pine Spikes

Boletes

Oak root fungus runs easily in the wet sand

Oak root fungus kills more than oaks

Live soil holds more water than 'dead' soil

Properties of water

Sticks together

Dissolves

Iron

Magnesium

Sodium

Zinc

Nitrogen

Cuts

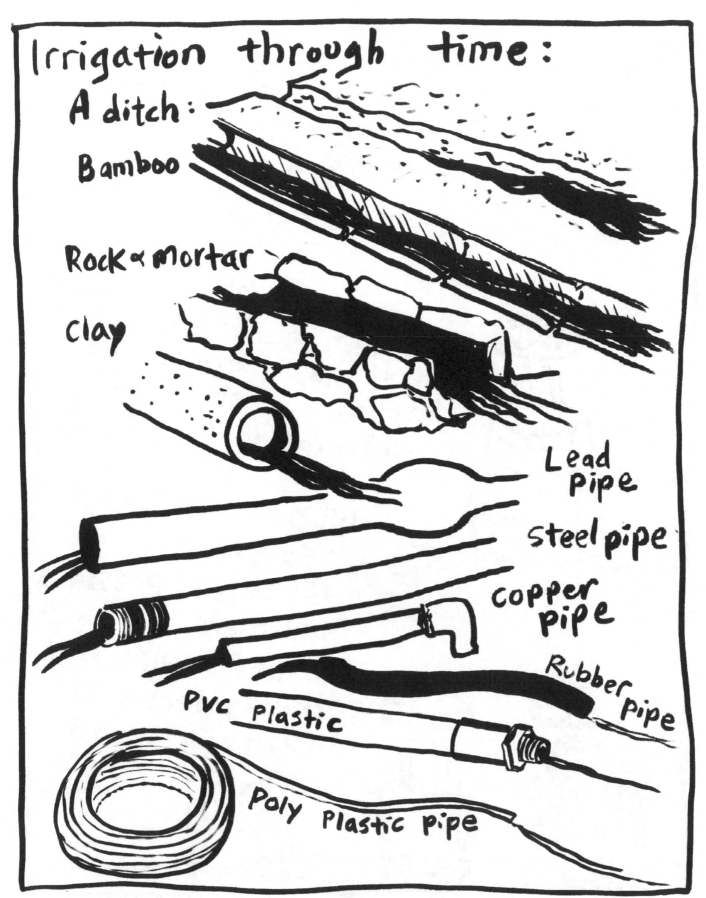

Problems with water valves:

Corrosion, rust, gunk, time: Valve gets stuck open, gets stuck closed, or gets stuck in the middle

Washer gets old, brittle, and broken

When valves are subject to repeated pressure hammers, on-off on-off switches, the system will rupture in weak spots.

Irrigation problems around trees:

How trees conserve water

Hang sideways

Breathe less

Drop leaves

Deep roots

small waxy leaves

Make friends with fungus

Aquaponics around the world

potato and pepper terraces in the Andes mountains

Aztec floating gardens of willow, corn & beans

Asian rice paddys

Cuttings : Ensure survival

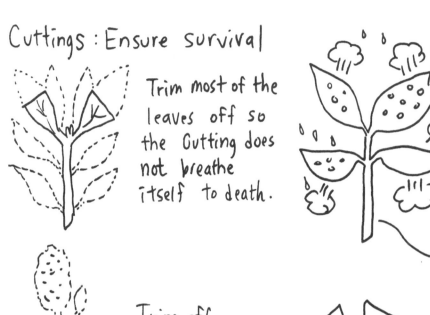

Trim most of the leaves off so the Cutting does not breathe itself to death.

Trim off the flowers & fruits.

Stomata (Breathing holes) – "I'm doin' my job!"

The cutting – "I don't have any roots yet! Can't suck up water efficiently! Gonna wilt and die!"

"I want my energy to go down & grow roots, not go up to make seeds and fruits! Get grounded first."

Cuttings = Timing, warmth, humidity

Some plants root in water in a week or two. Coleus. Willows.

Conifers can take a year to root, sitting patiently in a flat box of sand.

Subtropical Citrus grows roots fast in humid & warm conditions

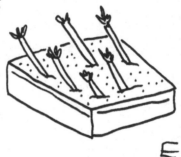

Some native California plants grow roots happily outdoors in cool San Francisco. Elderberry. Rose.

Cuttings: Energy stores & age

Too skinny—
not enough
energy stores
to grow roots

Too thick—
Hard to fit
in a container
of cutting mix.
Lot of inner
surface exposed
to the air.

Too young —
Sometimes prone
to rotting
instead of rooting.
wood tooooooo
soft.

Too old —
Old wood has a
harder time
regenerating &
growing roots

Cuttings: the cutting mix, the cutting medium

A mix with plenty of holes to grow roots easily, good access to air

A mix that holds water & nutrients, but is not goopy, compacted, hard, dense.

Big grains of sand

Lots of perlite, a little bit of Peat or coir coconut fiber

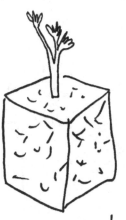

Rockwool

Cuttings: Rooting different plant parts

A square piece of Begonia leaf.

Matilija poppy a piece of root.

Kalanchoe leaf.

Chunk of Dracaena Stem

Cuttings: Hormones
  Tiny chemical messengers
  that help the plant —

Reach
towards
the light.

Ripen
fruits

Be patient and
wait to
grow
leaves.

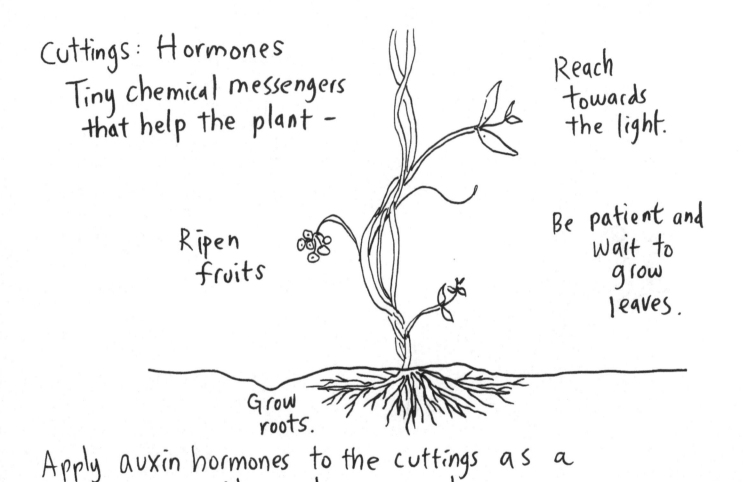

Grow
roots.

Apply auxin hormones to the cuttings as a
    liquid, powder, or a gel.

Cuttings: miscellaneous

Some growers scrape off parts of the stem skin to encourage more roots to grow.

other growers go all natural & use a solution of willow sticks as rooting hormone. Let the cuttings suck it up.

Patience & a green thumb are useful.

Try different plants, methods, timings to experiment. Some plants root easily 100% of the time, others are slow & difficult. Some cuttings thrive, others die. Talking to them and saying a prayer won't hurt.

Cuttings: General guidelines

 Use a dibble to make the hole. That way the tip of the cutting is not damaged by the sharp perlite.

 Put the base of cuttings close to the bottom. More nodes in the cutting mix means more chance for roots to grow.

 At least two or three nodes for roots to grow out of.

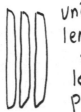 Uniformity in length & thickness looks professional.

 Pencil thickness has good energy stores to grow roots and leaves.

 Lots of cuttings together makes a little humid atmosphere to help each other from drying out & helping to root.

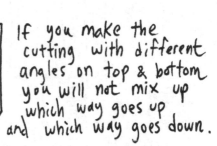 If you make the cutting with different angles on top & bottom you will not mix up which way goes up and which way goes down.

113

Harden off

Transplant Shock

How a tree dies: Myoporum laetum

How a tree dies: Pepper tree

How a tree dies: Coast live oak

There was once an oak, happy in the hills.

The oak got sold one day. Oak got scooped up, and moved to town.

Oak settled into the new home

The year-round irrigation was hard to get used to.

Every two weeks or so, Oak was whipped by little plastic strings.

Then came the fungus, sucking at the oak's root crown & trunk crotches.

The year the oak moths came, that was the last straw.

The end.

How a tree dies: Magnolia

How a tree dies: Monterey pine

Once upon a time, there was a baby pine.

In 80 years, the pine grew big and tall.

One day a twig beetle, covered with canker spores, paid a visit to ol' Pine.
Then an engraver beetle came also.
And a few more of their friends laid eggs in Pine.

The canker grew. It clogged channels.

Boring dust was left at Pine's base.

Pine tried to fight back for many years, but branches kept dying.

Pine got chopped down and chipped into mulch. So did the whole hillside of sick pines.

The end.

what tree parts are good to eat?

Da Sugary Sap

Long threads of Cellulose

Fruits

Brown blocks of lignins

Flower Petals

Leaves

Pollen & nectar

Roots

Ways pathogens travel:

In the wind and water

In spit

from flower to flower

on tools & in trucks

on animals

Ways pathogens enter trees:

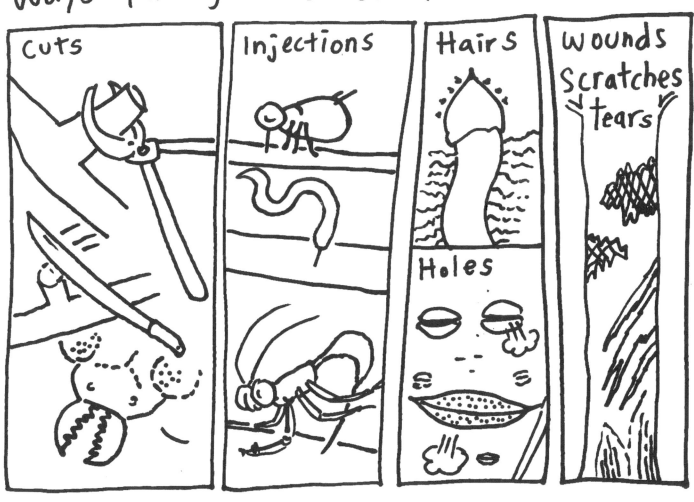

Fungus - fear cultures

English - Mushrooms!? Yucky Toad Stools!

"Fungus"?!
Everything dark & rotten.
Pure evil!!

Americans - Only the white buttons are safe. Stay in the grocery store, don't go to the woods!

Mushrooms are for hippies and immigrants. Or for flies and slugs. Stay away!!

Yum!

Peace bro!

Fungus - loving cultures

124

Fungus lifestyles in the garden

Fungus life cycle - Lower fungi

Mold spores land on edge of shower

Spores germinate and form threads of tubular branches called hyphae

A network of hyphae form an interconnected mass of mycelium

Mold oozes enzymes. The enzymes break down the caulk on the edge of the tub. Mold eats the plastic shower curtain and the paint on the walls.

The colony of fuzzy mold makes spores.

Mom says, "Enough! Time to clean the bathroom!"

Bathroom doors are opened to let air in. The fan is turned on. Bleach is applied. Prevent mold habitat, keep it dry!!!

Fungus life cycle - Higher Fungi

Stinkhorn spore germinates on some pine wood chips in the flower bed

White webs of stinkhorn mycelium soon cover the chips.

Wood is tasty!! Fungus breaks the wood down into carbon and phosphorus, nitrogen and potassium...

Then absorbs the nutrients!

With irrigation and rains, the mat of mushroom body grows and grows.

In the fall, the stinkhorn forms a round ball of a 'fruit', a mushroom!

The mushroom matures. It becomes an orange pink lattice with a brown goopy interior full of spores.

STINKY!!!

Flies come to check it out. Maybe it is a dead animal? A good place for baby maggots to feed? Spores attach to the flies. Dispersal of stinkhorn is successful!

Disease Caused by Fungus - Pine pitch canker

Pine tree twigs & branches all brown.

Piles of wood dust at the base of tree. Sores of bleeding sap on the trunk

The pine is sick. Who is the culprit?

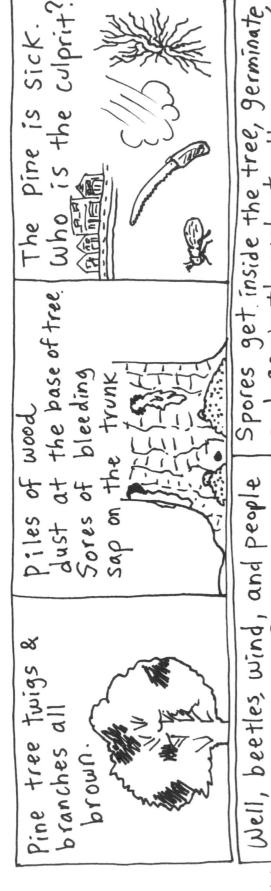

Well, beetles, wind, and people are carriers of Canker spores

Spores get inside the tree, germinate, and grow throughout the branches & trunk. They clog and kill the tree.

A New generation of young Pines grow up. Let's see who is resistant to the canker.

Trees are cut down and made into chips. Hopefully before they fall and hurt somebody

Fungus-identification

Color changes—
Does the mushroom stain different colors when scratched & bruised?

On the cap—
Lines & markings?
Scales or slime?
Hairs or bumps?

Under the cap—
Are there gills?
Teeth?
or
Spongy tubes?

What color are the spores?
Take a print!

where the Gill attaches to the stem—
Like this?

This?   Maybe this?

Stem—
Break it, twist it.
Is it string like fibers?
Crunchy like chalk?

Underground—
Is there a swollen lumpy base? A long root?

Fungus-identification : Partial & Universal veils

A veil covers the young mushroom's gills

PARTIAL VEIL

As the mushroom grows up, the veil breaks open

Mature spores fly out from the gills. A ring of veil tissue is left on the stem.

The ring!

A veil surrounds the whole mushroom in its 'egg' stage

UNIVERSAL VEIL

The mushroom matures, tearing the veil

RIP!

Little bits of veil are left on the cap & underground.

VOLVA!

Fungus identification - Two groups

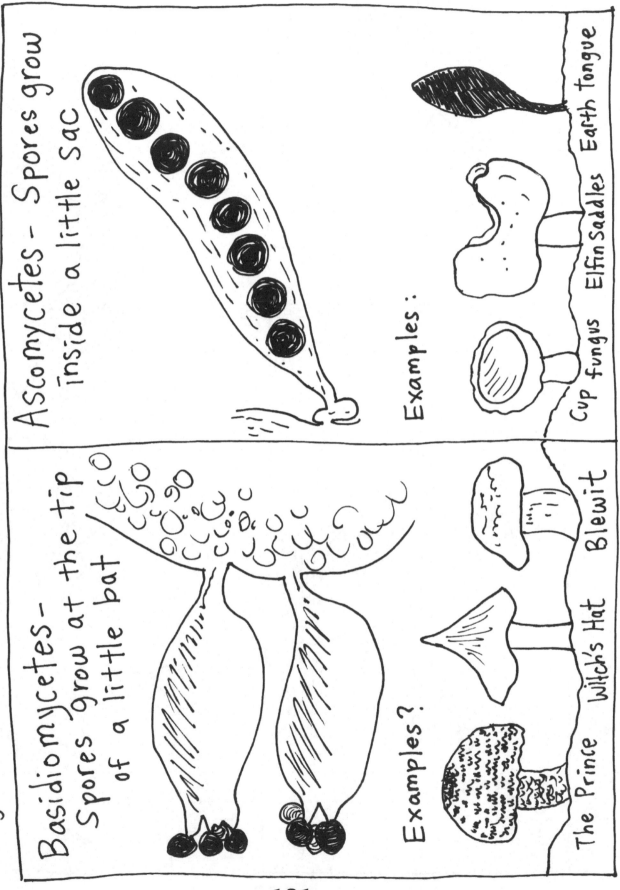

Ascomycetes - Spores grow inside a little sac

Examples:

Cup fungus Elfin Saddles Earth tongue

Basidiomycetes - Spores grow at the tip of a little bat

Examples?

The Prince Witch's Hat Blewit

Fungus ecology — ?/000 million years of diligent evolution

Decomposers & recyclers extraordinaire

Food for others

Hunters of worms, killers of trees

Link the earth together in mats and webs of relationships

Fungus ecology - Human relationships

Fungus toxicology - A case of Poisoning

Asian family settles in California

In the Pine Forest, he finds some fine white mushrooms

Pops goes out collecting mushrooms for dinner, in the park

The mushrooms look just like the ones in the rice paddies back home! Put them in the basket!

Mom cooks them up for dinner. A stir fry with some noodles, bok-choi, tofu, chicken, ginger, soy sauce, sesame oil. Yum! Everyone loves it.

Go to the hospital. Too late... Many tears are shed...

Half a day later, the family is not feeling too good.

Fungus toxicology – another case of poisoning

Expert mushroom hunters gather in the woods for a foray.

Dr. B is particularly keen on eating Caesar's amanita.

Hey!! There's a big patch of 'em!! All still in the egg stage. Yum! Grab 'em!

Got a whole basketful! Can't wait to eat them!!

A couple of death caps got mixed in with the bunch. One moment of careless sloppiness.

A nice grill, some butter & garlic.

Then, many hours later…

Perhaps I made a mistake…

WESTERN CONIFER SEED BUG Leptoglossus Occidentalis

In the winter, Leptoglossus occidentalis hibernates in a shelter.

Come May, Leptoglossus goes to feed on pine cones & pine shoots

When seeds develop inside female cones, Leptoglossus sticks its long tubular mouth part into the seeds.

Digestive enzymes dissolve the seed contents. Leptoglossus then sucks up the seed juice.

Leptoglossus lays eggs end to end from May-July on needles of pine.

Baby Leptoglossus nymphs feed, grow, and molt. Feed, grow, & molt.

When it begins to get cold, Leptoglossus leave the pine forests to rest and seek protection.

ROUND HEAD WOOD BORER IN THE LONGHORN BEETLE FAMILY

Females lay eggs in a crack or a cut slit of a tree.

Eggs hatch, larvae bore into the phloem tubes, and feed in the mine tunnels. Yum!!

After a while, larvae go deeper and feed on the sapwood. In a chamber at the end of its feeding tunnel, the larvae become pupae. Metamorphosis!!!

Mines get bigger, and are packed with larvae poop (frass).

The trees cry—"First the drought, then the root fungus, and now, the beetles!!!"

Out of the pupae emerges the adult. The adult feeds on plants, then goes looking for a mate.

Emergence holes

137

BLACK PINELEAF SCALE Nuculaspis californica

In early summer, mouthless males who live a day or two meet and mate with blind, legless females.

Female lays a bunch of eggs under her shell.

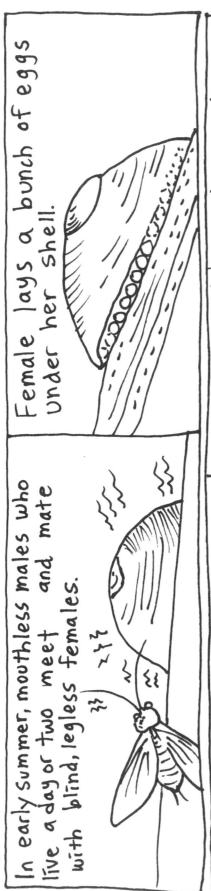

Little baby crawlers hatch, and go off to find a spot to feed.

Crawlers (nymphs) stick their mouth parts into a needle, and grow a waxy cover.

Females settle down, eat, shed skin, and grow bigger.

Males go into pupa stage under their shell, then come out with wings.

Predators & parasites feed on Nuculaspis.

People harvest dead trees on dusty roads, and spray insecticide on the scale insects. The insecticide also kills the beneficial insects. The result is more scale. Nuculaspis !!!

Make best use of weeds

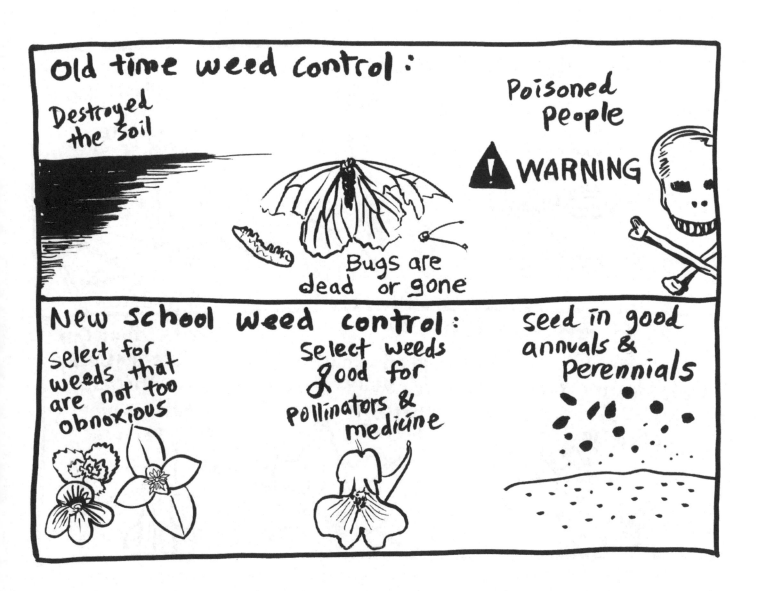

weeds to encourage:

plants with nectar, pollen, fruit & seeds.

Impatiens

Plants that behave. Plants that can cope with the surrounding conditions.

Lamium

Plants that protect other plants. Plants that cover the soil and regulate moisture and humidity.

Rubus

weeds to discourage:

plants that have too many successful offspring.

Ehrharta

plants that are bullys, robbers, and thieves.

Hedera

Plants that can injure passerbys with thorns, needles, spines, and poisons

Rubus

Nerves

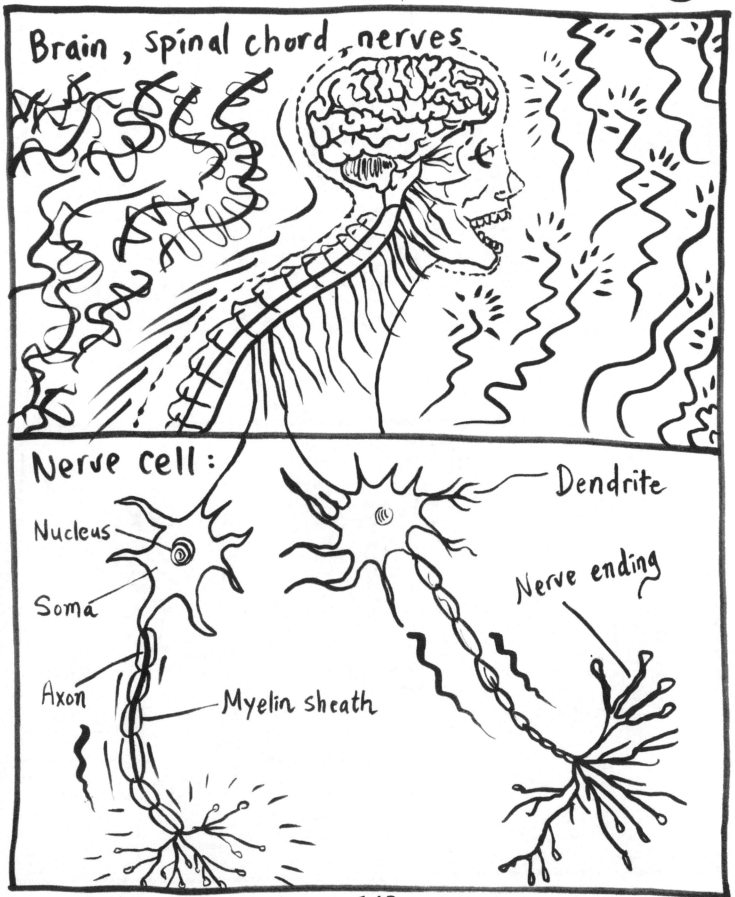

Brain, spinal chord, nerves

Nerve cell:

Nucleus

Soma

Axon — Myelin sheath

Dendrite

Nerve ending

Nerve system

Voluntary: Happens consciously. You think it, signal travels down the line, muscles move.

stand up.   sit down.   walk & run.

Involuntary: Operates unconsciously.

Digest food.   Breathe.   Cough & sneeze.

pee.   Vomit.   Get horny.   Heart beats.

Acetylcholine · Acetylcholine · Acetylcholine

Looks like this:

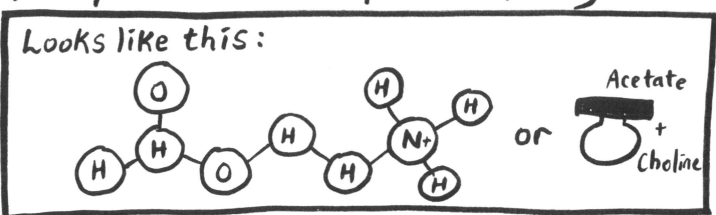

or

Acetate
+
Choline

Is a messenger called a neurotransmitter.
It activates muscles, brain, organs.

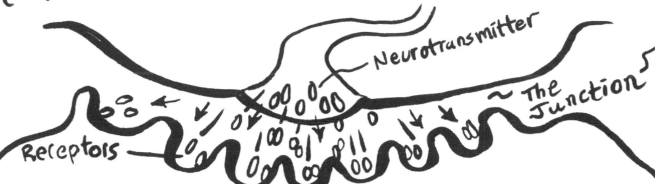

Neurotransmitter

~ The Junction

Receptors

At the neuro-muscular junction, signals are
exchanged. Binding of neurotransmitters at
the receptor site leads to muscle contraction.

Then comes Acetylcholinesterase. It inactivates
Acetylcholine. It clears and frees the
Acetylcholine from the synapse space.

Acetylcholine

Acetylcholinesterase

Acetate

choline

Neurotoxins

If Acetylcholinesterase is inhibited, stopped, the Acetylcholine builds up at the junction:

OVERLOAD! OVERLOAD!!

Muscle contract. Contract. Contract; Muscles do not relax. —Paralysis — Paralysis — paralysis— Can't breathe. No heart beating. Continuous stimulation → Fatal convulsions

Curare dart Poison blocks receptors. Dinner!

Nicotine mimics Acetylcholine at the receptors. Another puff...

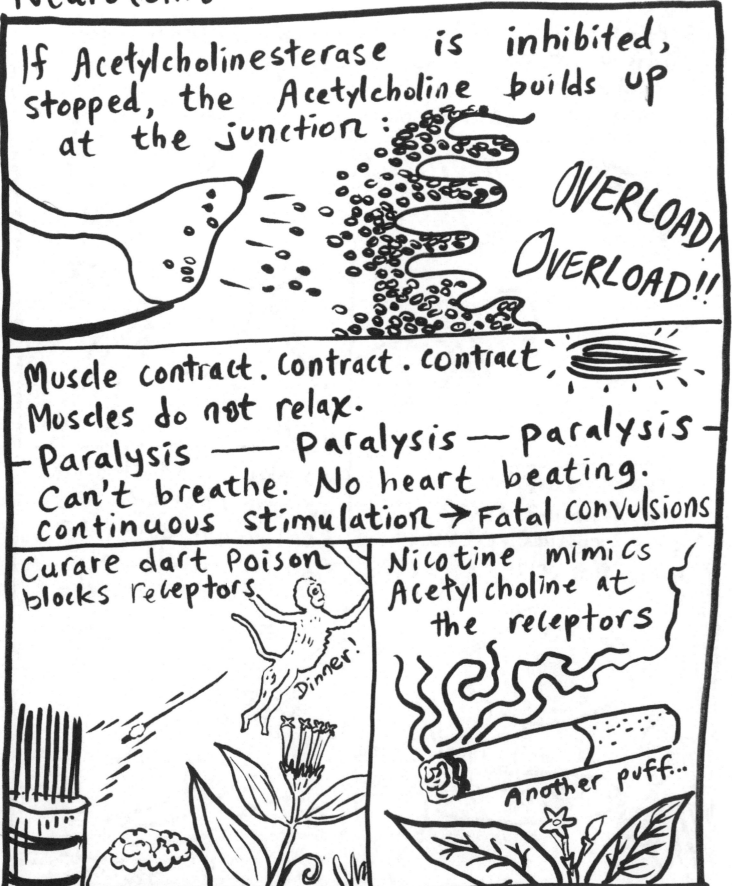

Botox - suppresses the release of Acetylcholine. Botulinum toxin relaxes muscles => results in smooth skin, less wrinkles

Black widow spider poison releases lots of Acetylcholine in the victim

Atropine can block Acetylcholine receptors, hence reduce nerve gas poisoning effects.

Atropa belladonna!

Mambas & rattlesnake venom destroy Acetylcholinesterase. Causing involuntary, long lasting muscle contraction.

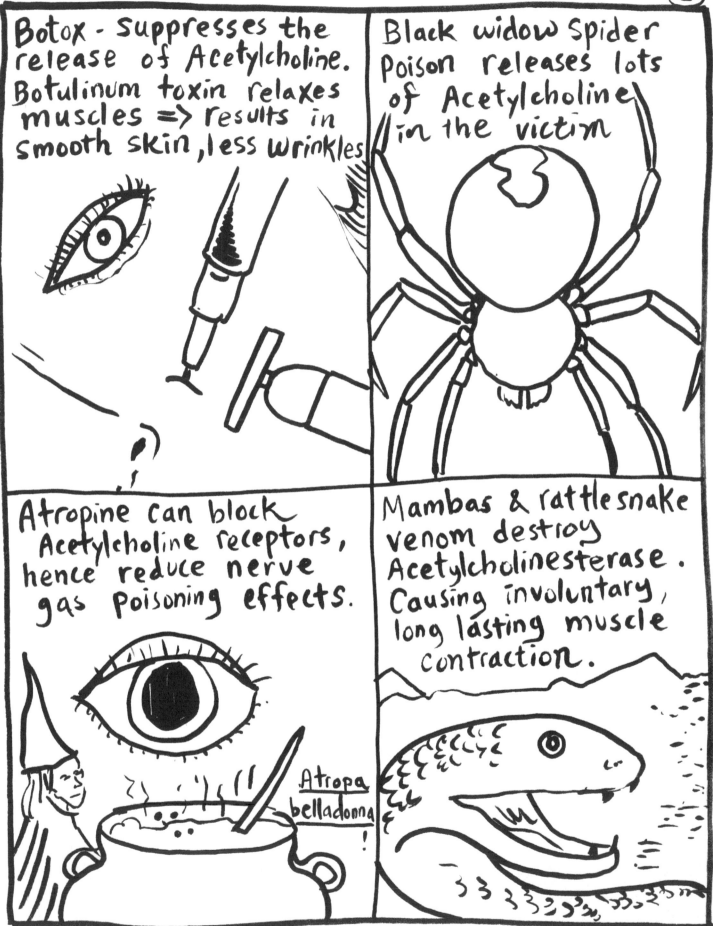

Pesticides and nerve poisons in horticulture & agriculture

Spinosad: Based on chemicals from the bacteria _Saccharopolyspora spinosa_. Binds to insect acetylcholine receptors.

cotton!

Dead tobacco budworm

Imidacloprid: Blocks receptors, prevents transmission between nerves → paralysis & death of insects.

Kill the thrips!!

But what about?...

Bzzzz

NeoNicotinid class

Dicrotophos: Inhibits acetylcholinesterase enzyme from breaking down acetylcholine.

my grains!

Rice bug alert!! organophosphate...

Dinotefuran: Disrupts insect nervous system. Inhibits acetylcholine receptors.

Argghh! Flea beetles on my lettuce!!

Shothole patterns

Try diatomaceous earth or beneficial nematodes

Neonicotinid class

Two types of acetylcholine receptors: ⑧

Muscarinic: 🌙
Named for the fly agaric mushroom *Amanita* *muscaria*

Muscarinic acetylcholine receptors are found in heart tissues, secretion glands, and smooth muscles (e.g. stomach, intestines, bladder)

Nicotinic:
Named for the tobacco plant *Nicotiana*

Nicotinic acetylcholine receptors are found in muscles; the brain; from the spine out to organs.

Where do many house plants come from?

From the shade of the jungle

To the cave of wood & stone

151

Why houseplants are prone to dying and disease.

Too dry. Heater is on.

Too wet. Water it too much. Drown it.

Potting soil is all peat or all bark, with little perlité or pumice.

No drainage
No aeration ⇒

Potting soil is old and rotted & decomposed

NO root space ⇒

Low light is not NO LIGHT

The air is too still.

Why are houseplants good for human health?

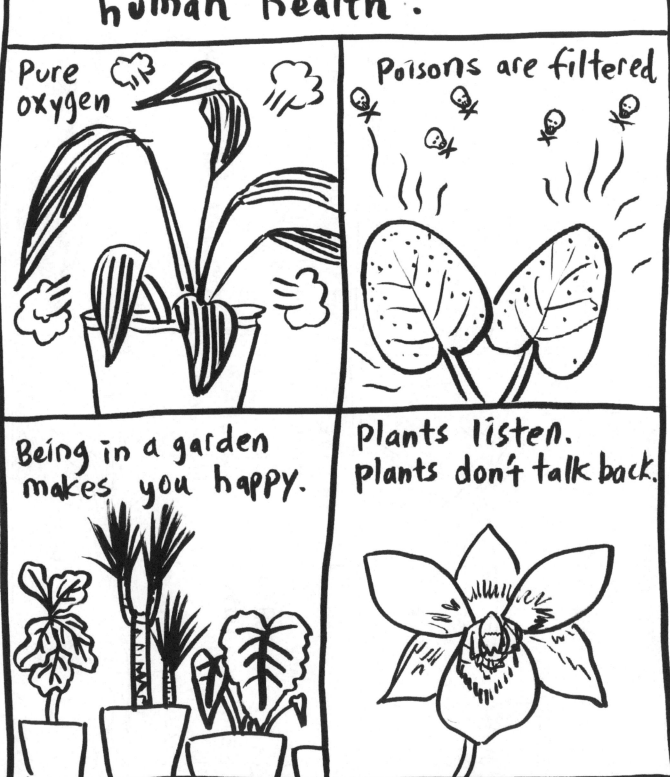

Pure oxygen

Poisons are filtered

Being in a garden makes you happy.

Plants listen. Plants don't talk back.

In the water around the lake edge was a grassy looking plant. It was triangular and not round in cross section. It had a pithy Styrofoam center instead of being hollow. It is a plant in the **Sedge** Family.

Grandma peeled the skin of the Chinese waterchestnut and ate them. **Sedge** again!!

As we walked around Lake Merced, People hit white balls with sticks on short neat grass. **High maintenance grass.** It needs mowing, watering, fertilizing, aerating, & spraying.

At the taco joint I drank horchata. Agua frescas! The flavor comes from the tubers of chufa. Another **Sedge!**

Panel 1 (top left):

Mr. Yamamoto threw me down on the mat of tatami. Sensei, what kind of throw was that? I saw a flash of fibers woven in the mat. More **Rushes**!!

Panel 2 (top right): ③

At the market, next to the live tanks of sturgeon & crab, there were long stalks of cane. A tall grass of sugar. A **cash crop grass**.

Panel 3 (bottom left):

Went hiking to San Bruno Mountain. At the base of Buckeye Canyon, in the low wet spots, clumps of green shoot up next to the willows. **Rushes!**

Panel 4 (bottom right):

Checking the surf at the beach. All blown out. Afternoon onshores. **Dune grasses** ran in all directions as sand tried to swallow them up.

In Visitacion Valley and McLaren Park, Fourth of July fireworks burned the grasslands. Sprouting up were **bunch grasses** of purple needle grass and California oat grass. Was that a herd of antelope?!

On Bayview Hill, where the moist soil met the edge of the cherry forest, I lay my head down on the tufted hair grass for a nap. A **Caespitose grass.**

Grandma says "Stay for dinner, eat the vegetables, not just the rice." Rice. Oryza. Oh tasty **edible grass!**

Up in Sacramento, Catherine grew Citrus, hot peppers, and **lemon grass.** She gave me a bowl of rice noodle soup, barbecue chicken feet, and a shot of whisky. I saw angels!

157

Bruce's pet lizard got a foxtail stuck in its eye. Wahhhh! Off to the Veterinarian we go. **Grass awns.** Poky and problematic!

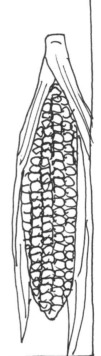

In the aisles of the super market, one grass ruled over them all. The one with fat seeds that stay together and don't shatter. The one that feeds pigs & people alike. **Sacred grass.**

The native people returned to colonize the world. They wove maiden hair ferns into deer grass stems. They wove in all the cultures and all beings. **Basket grass.**

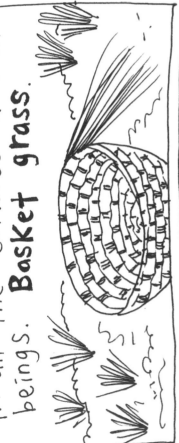

Bird seed scattered and sprouted by the sidewalk. Up came a corn looking thing. But smaller. Millet! A **drought-tolerant grass.**

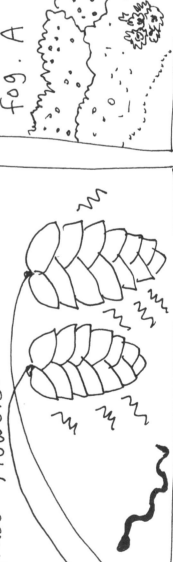

While I finished wrestling the erharta grass out of the ground, its enormous root system surprised me and sent me tumbling down the hill. A very **fibrous root**

On the north slope of Mt. Davidson, Footsteps-of-Spring parties with Angelica and Huckleberry. California fescue drinks some more fog. A **Cool Season Grass.**

Buffalo grass covers the sod house with **stolons**. It is a **warm season grass** that can take the heat! Tatanka!

Quaking grass flowers hang down like rattlesnake tails and rustle in the wind. Pendant **spikelets** of grass flowers.

Girdling root

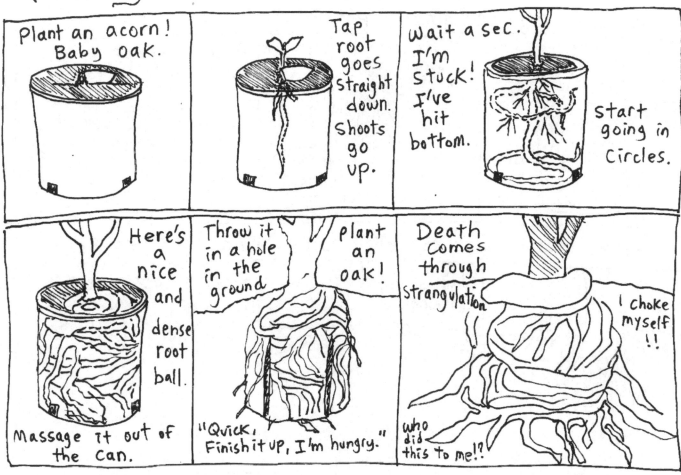

Planting technique : Trees

Plant with the container's potting soils intact

Clay — Bark & Sand — Clay

"What's with the roots in the bark?"

"Where you come from?"

"I get the feeling that I don't belong"

A day of hot sun - Irrigation breaks

Ja ja ja

Food!

Ha ha ha

Remove some or most of the container potting soils

Whew! Made it out of the container!

Tree Support & Staking: How does a tree grow strong?

Safety pruning in S.F. - Gardening in the City:

Sucker - what is a sucker?

Pollarding Sycamores —

Vista pruning?
shoots for fuel & baskets?

166

Crown thinning a bottlebrush tree

Pruning: which style is better?

Topping in San Francisco I

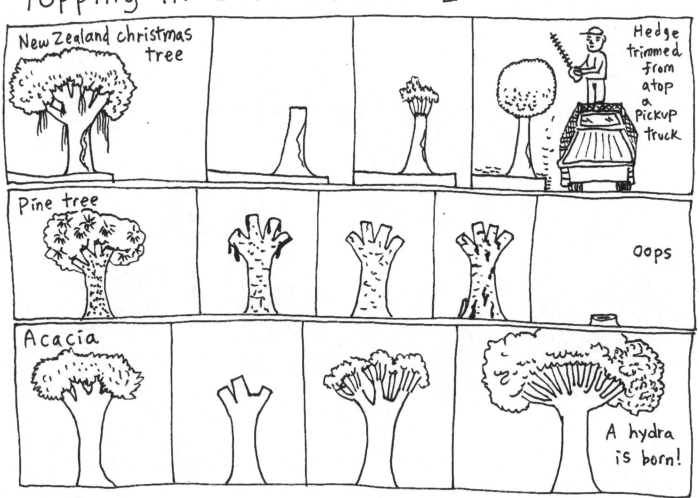

Topping in San Francisco II

Timing of pruning: Every tree is SPECIAL

when do you prune a tree in San Francisco?

Crown reduction
What's the best way to lower the height of a tree?

172

Lion tails:
On what plant is 'lion tail style' pruning 'appropriate'?

(Trick question)

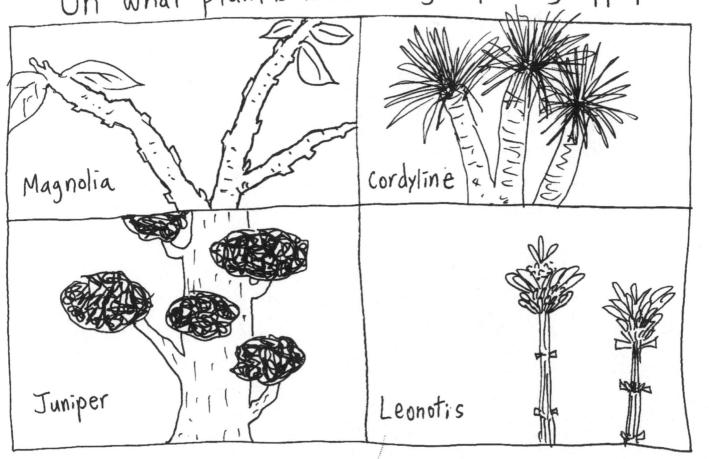

Magnolia

Cordyline

Juniper

Leonotis

CAMELLIA FLOWER FORMS:

SINGLE

SEMI-DOUBLE

ANEMONE DOUBLE

NEAT ROW OF PETALS ON THE OUTSIDE

A CENTER OF PETALLOIDS

AND STAMENS

PEONY DOUBLE

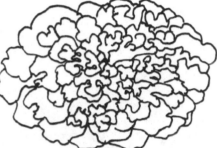

BILLOWY UNEVEN MASS OF PETALS & PETALLOIDS

ROSE-DOUBLE

PETALS SURROUND AND OVERLAP EACH OTHER THE CENTER IS HIDDEN

FORMAL DOUBLE

GEOMETRIC PETALS UNFURL

STAMENS ARE TUCKED IN THE MIDDLE

CAMELLIA SPECIES:

C. SINENSIS

THE CAMELLIA COMMONLY
DRANK AS 'TEA'

SIMPLE SMALL WHITE & YELLOW
FLOWERS

C. JAPONICA

THE COMMONLY GROWN
ORNAMENTAL CAMELLIA
LARGE BEAUTIFUL FLOWERS
IN MANY COLORS

C. SASANQUA

山茶花 = SA ZAN KA

= MOUNTAIN TEA FLOWER

C. RETICULATA

DULL GREEN LEAVES
VEINS LIKE A NET = RETICULATE
GROWS TO THE SIZE OF A
BIG TREE WITH TIME. 50'+!!!

176

CAMELLIA SPECIES:

C. OLEIFERA

SEEDS ARE SQUEEZED
TO MAKE OIL
FOR COOKING AND
FOR PRESERVING WOOD

C. YUNNANENSIS

CHINA

BANGLADESH

INDIA

YUNNAN
PROVINCE

BURMA

LAOS

THAILAND

VIETNAM

C. CHRYSANTHA
THE GOLDEN CAMELLIA
FLOWERS ARE YELLOW

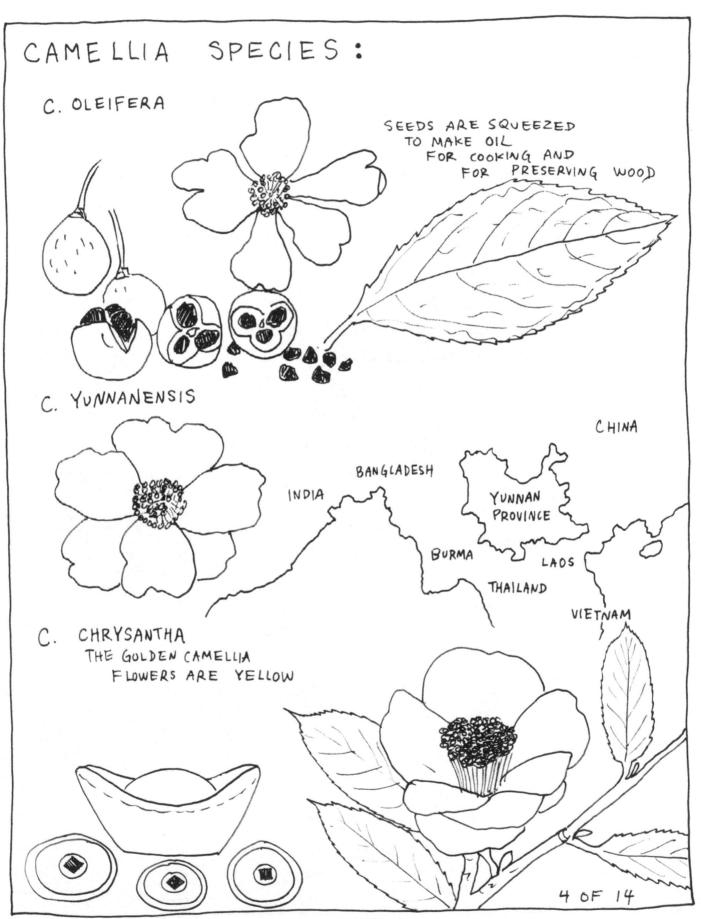

TEA
CHA

FLOWER
HUA

CAMELLIAS:

EVERGREEN   SHRUB AND SMALL TREE

LEAVES ALTERNATELY ARRANGED

SIMPLE GLOSSY SERRATED LEAF

LARGE FLOWERS
POLLINATED BY BEES

DRY CAPSULE FRUIT
WITH SEEDS IN
1-5 CHAMBERS

6 OF 14

179

椿

TSUBAKI

WHAT IS PICKED?

TWO LEAVES AND A BUD

WHO PICKS IT?

A PERSON WITH A HAT AND A BASKET

THE COST OF A CUP OF TEA, 1801:
SILVER TO BUY BUNDLES OF TEA LEAVES

LABOR TO
WORK THE SUGAR CANE FIELDS

A PORCELAIN CUP OF
TEA & SUGAR
IN AN ENGLISH PARLOUR

11 OF 14

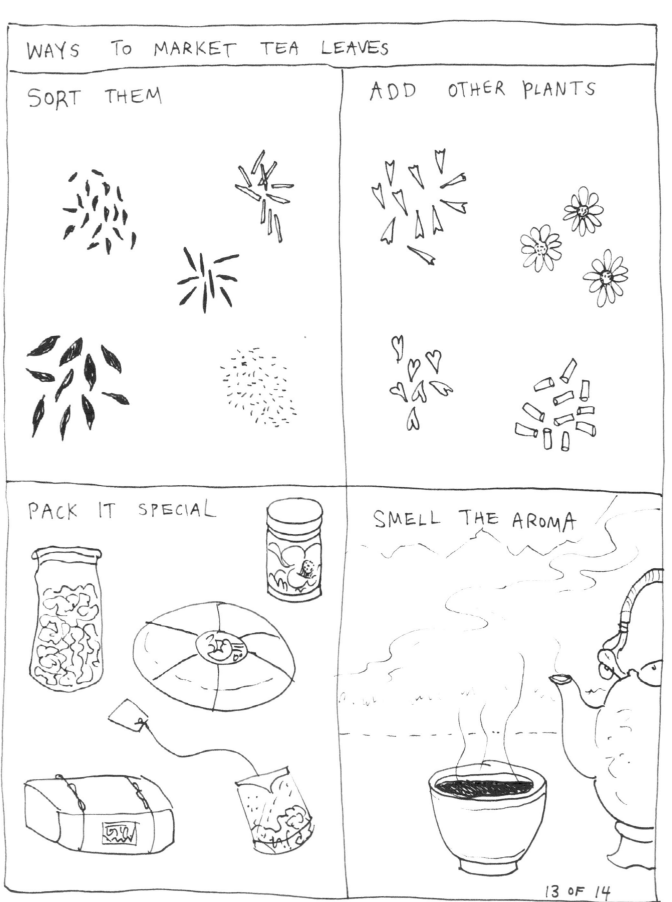

WAYS TO MARKET TEA LEAVES

SORT THEM

ADD OTHER PLANTS

PACK IT SPECIAL

SMELL THE AROMA

TEA PARTY:

FURNITURE

TEA SET

ACTIVITIES

FRIENDS

14 OF 14

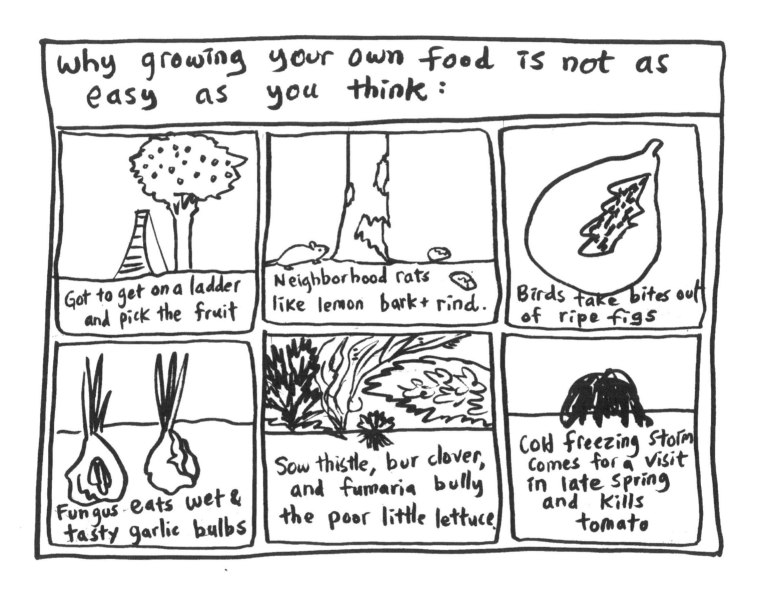

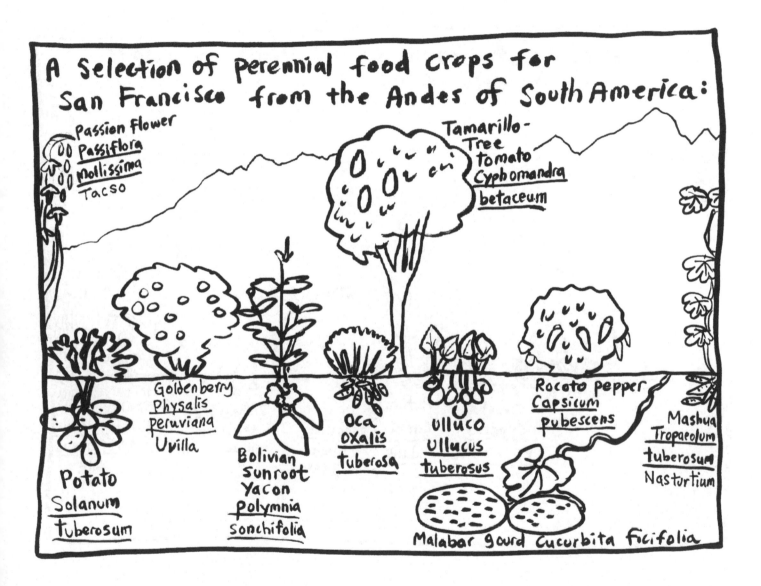

A Selection of perennial food crops for San Francisco from the Andes of South America:

Passion flower
Passiflora
mollissima
Tacso

Tamarillo-Tree tomato
Cyphomandra
betaceum

Goldenberry
Physalis
peruviana
Uvilla

Potato
Solanum
tuberosum

Bolivian sunroot
Yacon
polymnia
sonchifolia

Oca
Oxalis
tuberosa

Ulluco
Ullucus
tuberosus

Rocoto pepper
Capsicum
pubescens

Mashua
Tropaeolum
tuberosum
Nasturtium

Malabar gourd Cucurbita ficifolia

189

A selection of food crops that do well in San Francisco:

Autumn berry
Eleagnus
umbellata

Fuchsia berry

Chufa
Cyperus
esculentus

Achira
Canna
edulis

Uñi
Ugni
molinae
Chilean
guava

Dichelostemma
capitatum
Blue
dicks

Hoja
santa
Piper
auritum

Phaseolus
coccineus
Red
runner
bean

190

The plant <u>Brassica oleracea</u> has many forms:

Cabbage makes a round head of leaves.

Kohlrabi has a swollen round stem.

Cauliflower has a round ball of young flower shoots.

Collards: "No heads or balls, just tasty leaves."

All are <u>Brassica oleracea</u>!
Let's store starch in different places.

Crop rotation:

Heavy & light feeders. Take turns!

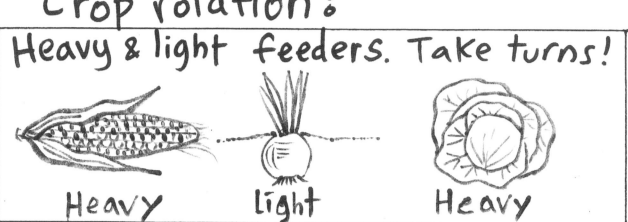

Heavy   light   Heavy

Reduce pest buildups:

ENOUGH   ROOT MAGGOTS!

Use legumes to add soil nitrogen.

Give it a rest, will ya?

Cold Hardiness - when it gets cold around here...

Wind tolerance : San Francisco is a windy place

Growth rate & old age

Form

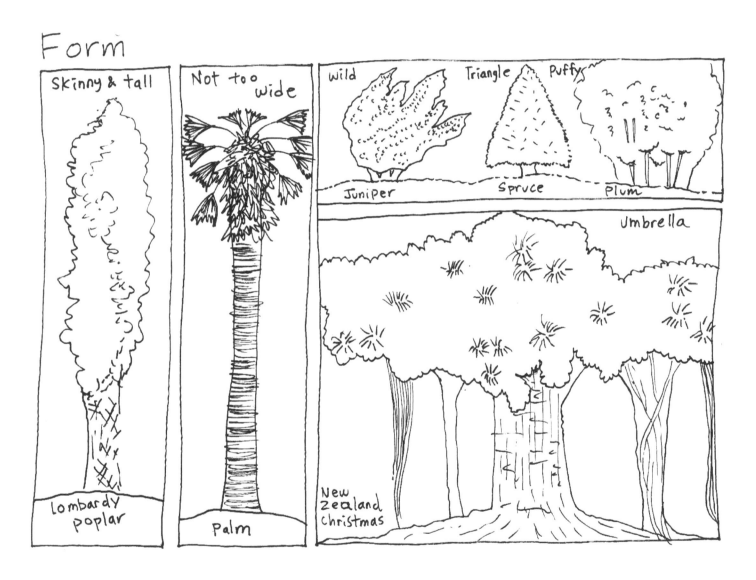

Skinny & tall

Lombardy poplar

Not too wide

Palm

Wild — Juniper

Triangle — Spruce

Puffy — Plum

Umbrella

New Zealand Christmas

Pest resistance : what tree can resist – ?

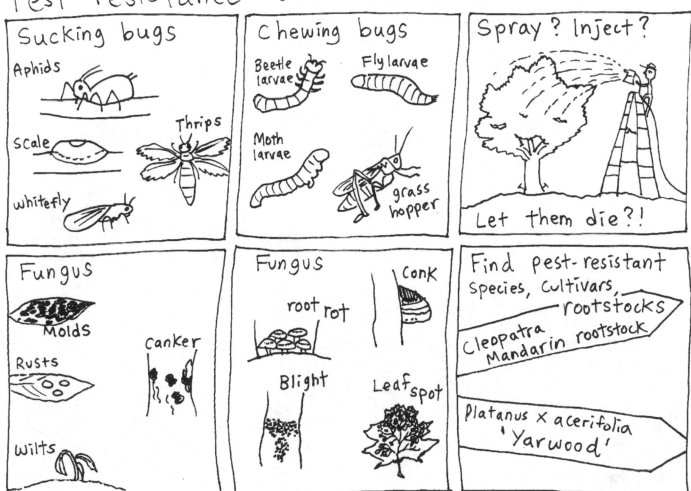

Sucking bugs
Aphids
scale
whitefly
Thrips

Chewing bugs
Beetle larvae
Fly larvae
Moth larvae
grass hopper

Spray? Inject?
Let them die?!

Fungus
Molds
Rusts
canker
Wilts

Fungus
root rot
Conk
Blight
Leaf spot

Find pest-resistant species, cultivars, rootstocks
Cleopatra Mandarin rootstock
Platanus x acerifolia 'Yarwood'

Messy and Smelliness

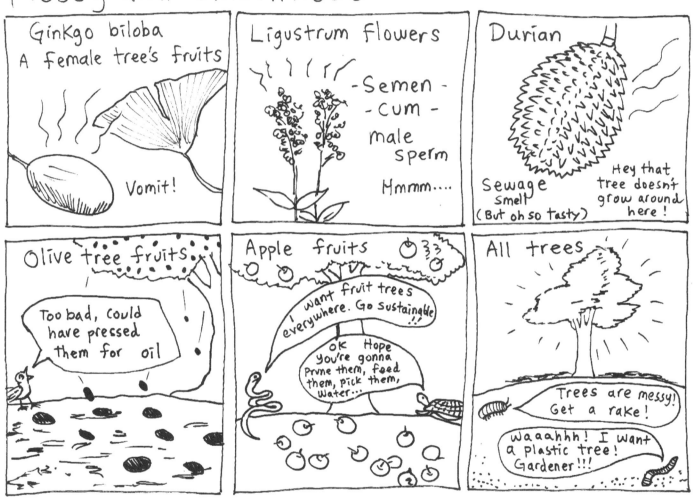

Native or Exotic - who draws the lines? State? County? Hill? Year?

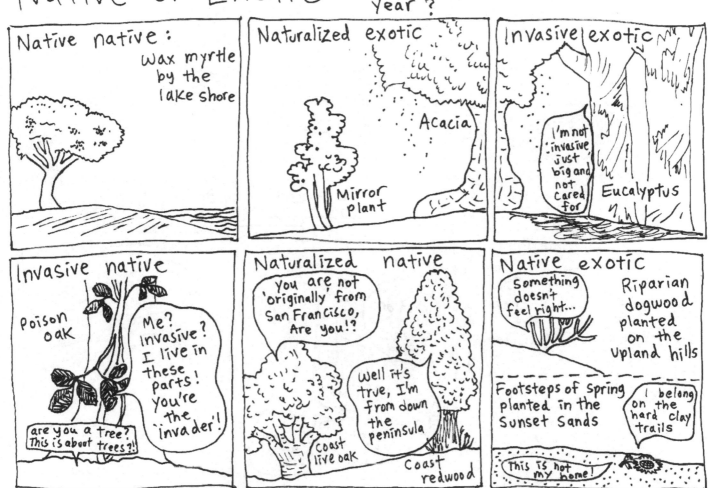

Invasive roots

Tolerate Pollution

Sun & Shade

North side Fuchsia Paniculata

This is a good place for me

North side Azara

I grow, but have few flowers ... Need more sun!

East side Fig

My fruits!! where's the Southern exposure?

West Side Monterey Cypress

South Side lemon

Sugar & Sun!

Southside Euphorbia

Happiness is the light

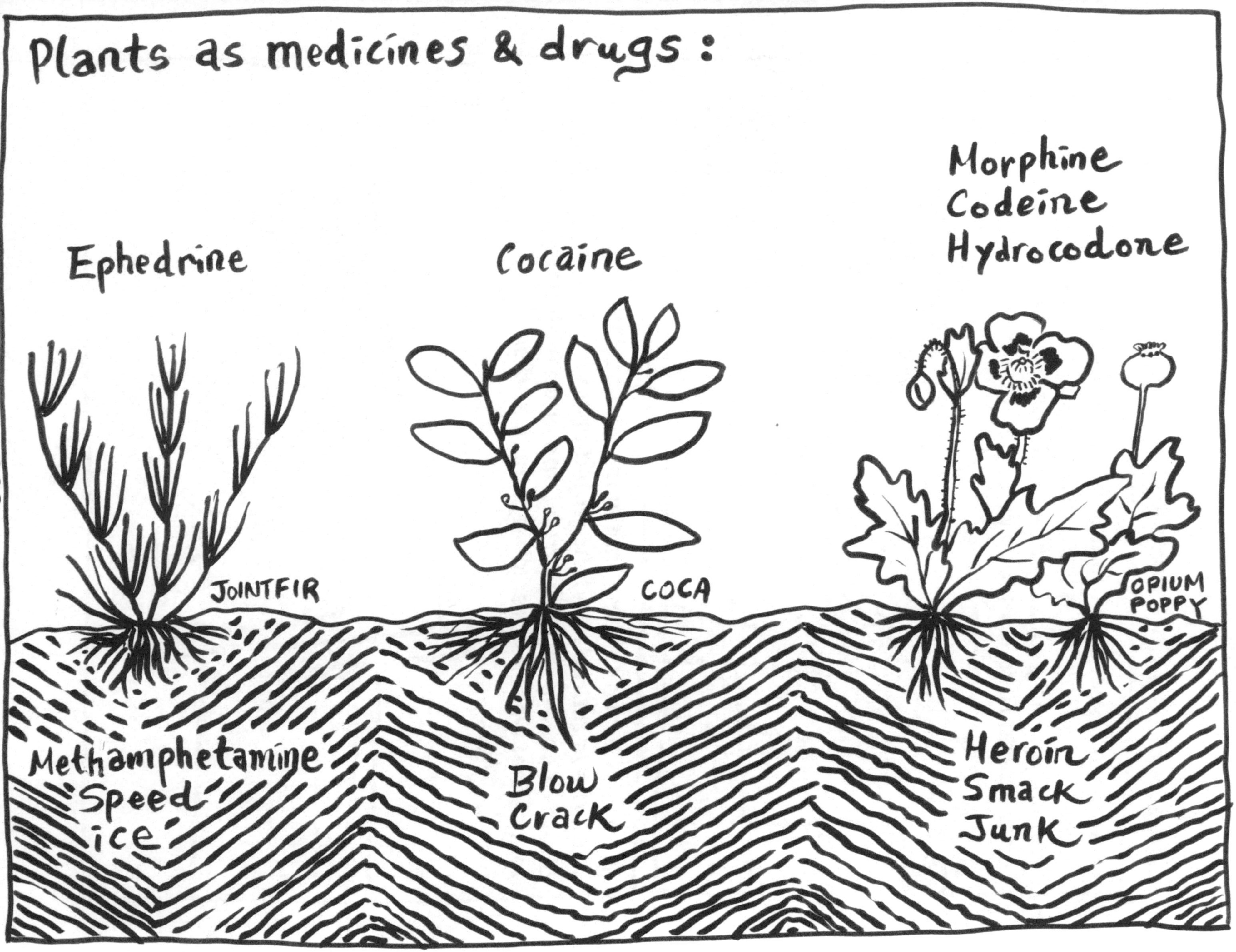

Plants as medicines & drugs:

Morphine
Codeine
Hydrocodone

OPIUM POPPY

Heroin
Smack
Junk

Cocaine

COCA

Blow
Crack

Ephedrine

JOINTFIR

Methamphetamine
"Speed"
"ice"

203

There is a sweet drink that bubbles and fizzes called Coca-Cola. It is said that drinking it makes you happy and probably beautiful, too. My doctor from Puerto Rico is in love with the soda.

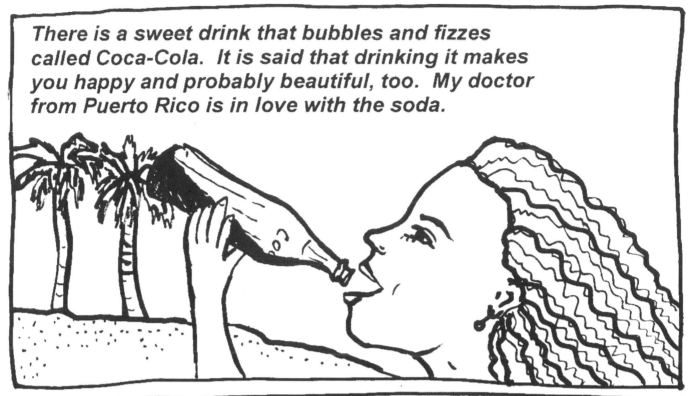

My friend Steve told me that when he used to work (he is retired now), he would bring a 2 liter bottle of coca-cola in his truck and chug it all day long. That was his breakfast, lunch, and snack too.

After doing this awhile, he got diabetes. All that sugar swimming around in his blood could not get broken down and used up. The sweet sugars ended up being a nasty poison.

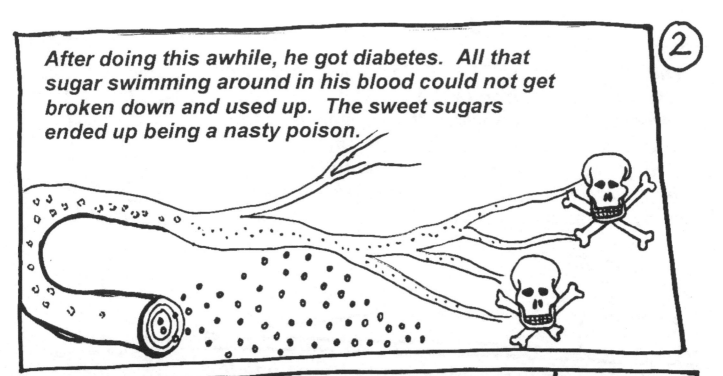

Diabetes is called sugar pee sickness in Chinese (meaning if you taste the pee it is sweet). You inject yourself with insulin to help break down the sugars. If diabetes gets bad, your body's filter, the kidneys, stop working. Then, you have to filter your blood with a machine every few weeks or so.

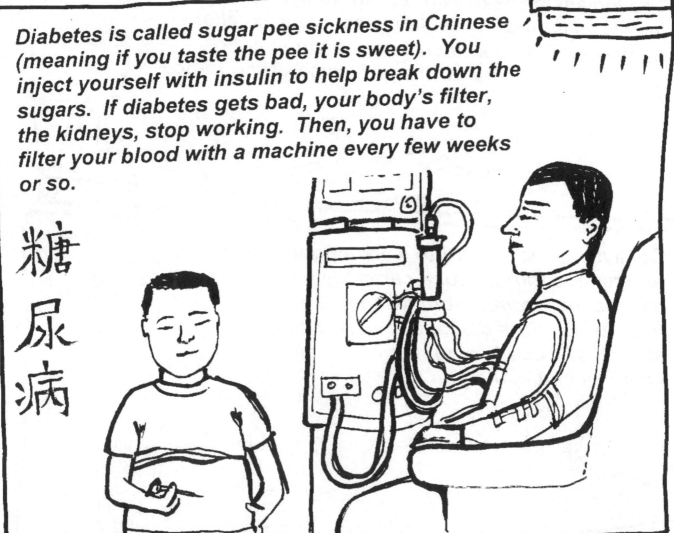

糖
尿
病

The tasty flavor of Coca-Cola comes from two plants. The first one is the coca plant. Coca is native to South America. It grows around the Andes Mountains with the Incas and lamas. It also grows down in the wet steamy lowlands of the Amazon jungle. It is a small green shrub with shiny leaves and red berries.

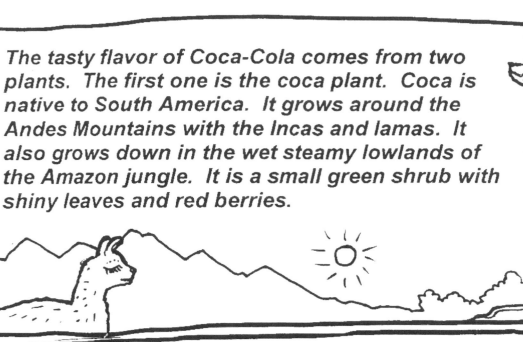

The Indians grow the coca plant to consume the leaves as a ritual food. It has so many excellent qualities that it is known as the Divine Leaf of Immortality, the leaf of the gods, and other names like that.

Coca leaf enables you to work longer and tolerate hunger and thirst. Coca cures the headaches and nausea that come from living in the high mountains. This disease is known as altitude sickness. Coca is a source of protein and vitamins that make you strong.

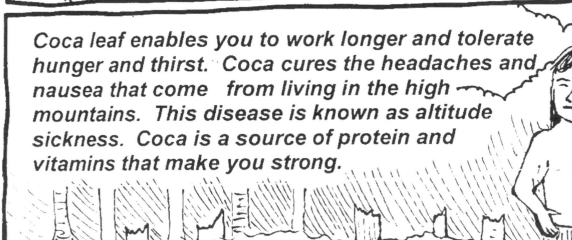

Indians roast the coca leaves and then chew them with some lime made from limestone or burnt plant ashes. The two substances go well together as a lumpy quid on the side of the cheek.

Leaves are exchanged as a friendly gesture, chewed in contemplation, and drunk as a tea. Every person's homegrown coca leaf tastes a little different.

Back in the day, when the Spanish people arrived by boats to South America, they learned about the coca plant. They thought that the plant was very useful, and grew it in plantations.

In the highlands of the Andes where the condors fly, Quichua Indians lived amongst the clouds and in the missions. They worked hard, ate too much coca leaf, and not enough other foods. They became unhealthy and malnourished.

In the lowland jungles, the rainforest Indians ate coca leaf, but also went fishing and hunting. They collected wild fruit, and tended gardens of chili, manioc, corn, plantain, and yucca. They stayed in good shape.

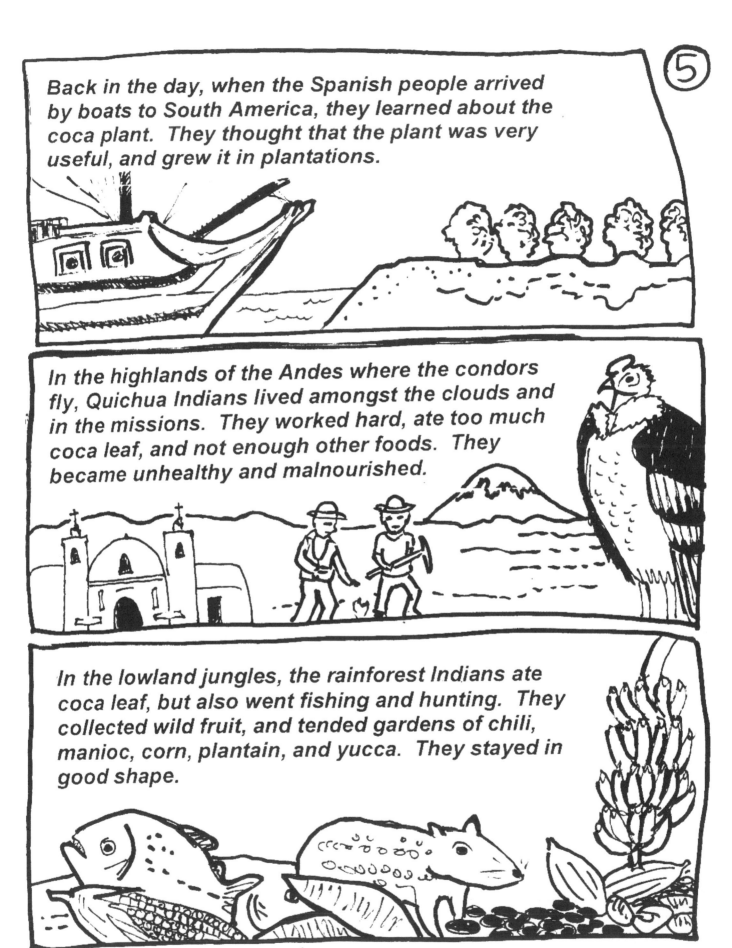

A German doctor isolated the chemical responsible for the magical effects of coca, and named it cocaine. Scientists discovered that the chemical could be extracted, taken out of the plant, and concentrated into a fine white powder.

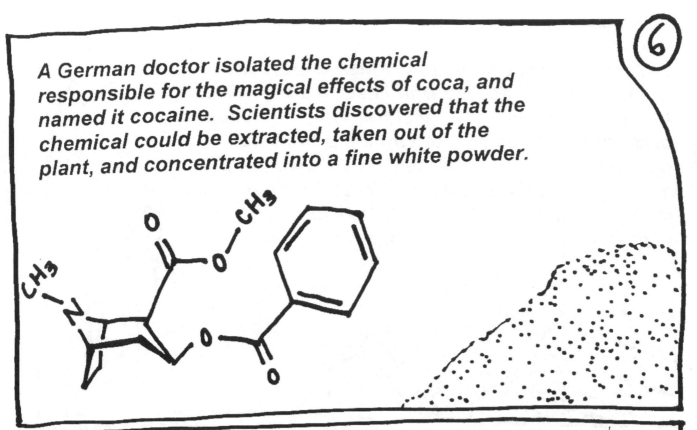

Cocaine began to be used by doctors in surgery when they cut open patients. Cocaine is an anesthesia, a drug that can numb you and make you feel no pain.

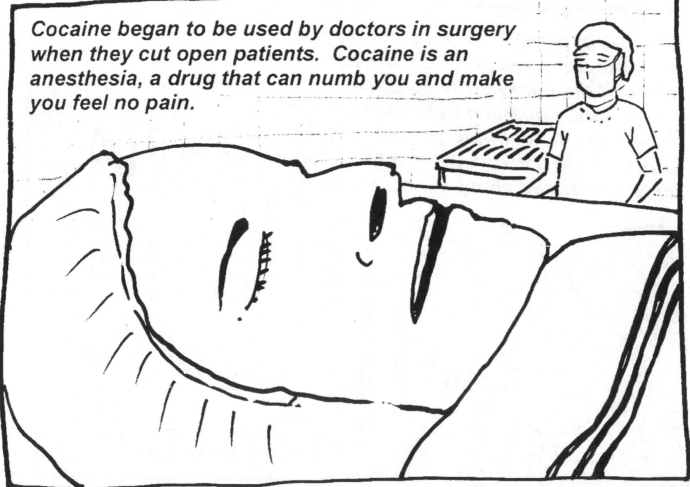

With time, cocaine became a fashionable drug among wealthy people who liked to party. Rock musicians, movie and TV stars, business people, and politicians all snorted up lines of white powder through their noses. With cocaine, they no longer felt the pressure, stress, and alienation that came with being a high-class personality. It sent the mind to another place.

Cocaine became a hit drug among poor people who wanted to escape from the hardness and grime of the angry streets. Cocaine was mixed with baking soda and sold as little rocks for people to smoke in pipes. In the parks and street corners little packets were sold under the domino table, or passed along in secret handshakes.

Drugs are popular, and are worth a lot of money. It is a time and work intensive process to grow coca plants, take out the cocaine, and sell it in underground markets. There are many middlemen merchants all along the way. The selling of cocaine is illegal in most countries, so it has to be smuggled and secretly passed across borders on airplanes, trucks, and trains; and inside the colons of people too.

With the money from selling cocaine, people became rich. They bought guns and people. They bought high-rise buildings and mansions.

211

Concentrated cocaine is not the same as whole leaf of coca. One snort of cocaine powder may be 20 grams of actual cocaine. That amount is in 300 days of chewing coca leaves as a ritual food.

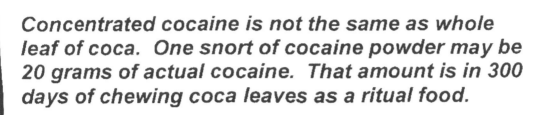

The second plant flavoring in the old time Coca Cola was the cola plant. Cola is a tree from the rainforests of West Africa, it is in the same family as cotton, okra, and hibiscus. Within the bitter seeds is caffeine.

Yes, you know caffeine. Caffeine is in coffee, in tea, in yerba mate, and in guarana. Caffeine is a stimulant. It makes you get up and go!

The nuts are roasted and powdered or chewed. They are added to tea, milk, or cereals.

Well, there is no more cocaine in Coca-Cola. That was outlawed back in the early 1900's. And there is no kola nut either. Instead, there is sugars from corn, vanilla from the fruit and seeds of an orchid, cinnamon from the bark of a tree, and other flavorful plants.

Like many substances - little bit, no problems. Too much - sickness and death. The end.

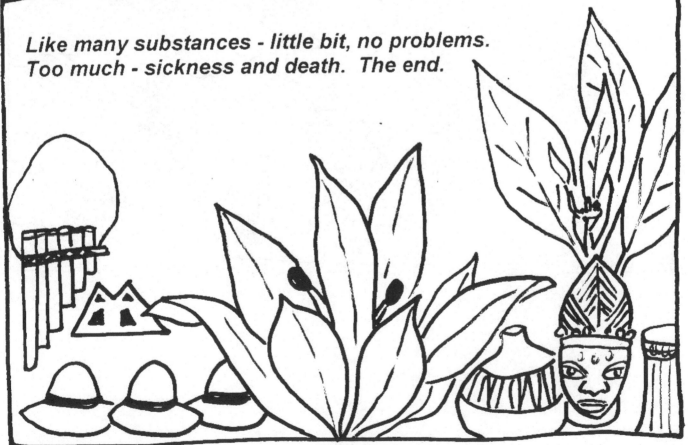

Pilgrimage to Wirikuta

Singing rain goddess

Sun archer

Desert child of eagle & agave

Friends of amanita & nightshade

06·11·2016

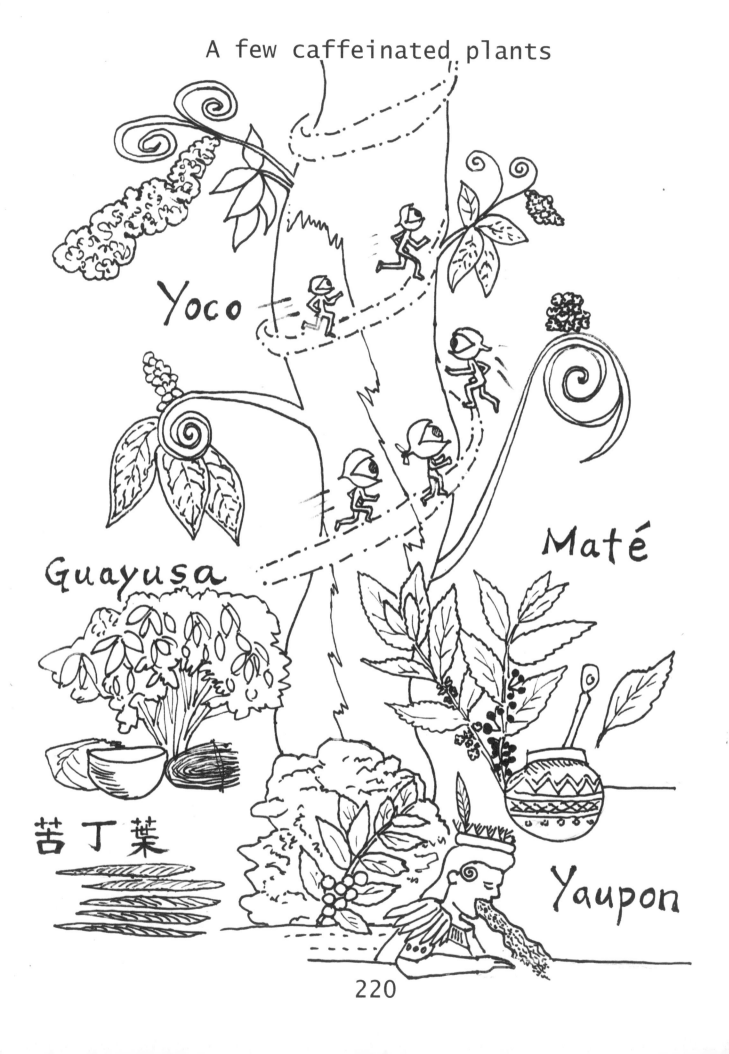

A few caffeinated plants

Yoco

Guayusa

苦丁葉

Maté

Yaupon

01-20-2013

Sun father paints the river rocks

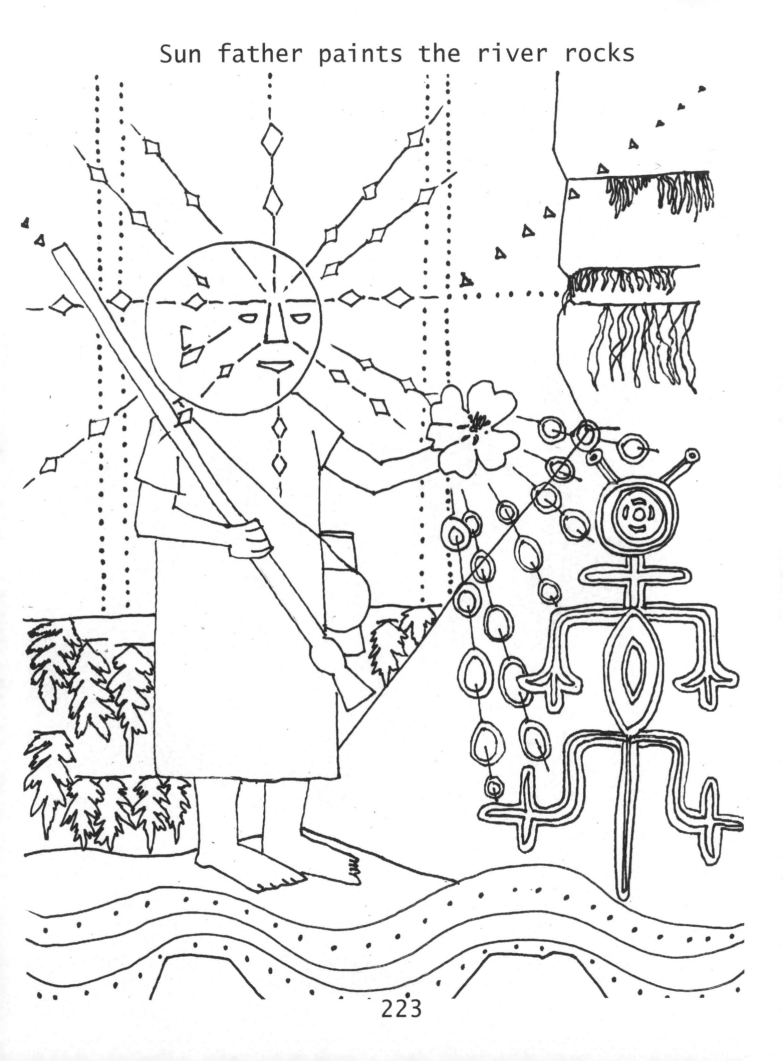

Where the Andes meets the Amazon

Milky way messengers